Globalization: A Very Short Introduction

VERY SHORT INTRODUCTIONS are for anyone wanting a stimulating and accessible way into a new subject. They are written by experts, and have been translated into more than 45 different languages.

The series began in 1995, and now covers a wide variety of topics in every discipline. The VSI library currently contains over 700 volumes—a Very Short Introduction to everything from Psychology and Philosophy of Science to American History and Relativity—and continues to grow in every subject area.

Very Short Introductions available now:

ABOLITIONISM Richard S. Newman
THE ABRAHAMIC RELIGIONS
    Charles L. Cohen
ACCOUNTING Christopher Nobes
ADDICTION Keith Humphreys
ADOLESCENCE Peter K. Smith
THEODOR W. ADORNO
    Andrew Bowie
ADVERTISING Winston Fletcher
AERIAL WARFARE Frank Ledwidge
AESTHETICS Bence Nanay
AFRICAN AMERICAN HISTORY
    Jonathan Scott Holloway
AFRICAN AMERICAN RELIGION
    Eddie S. Glaude Jr
AFRICAN HISTORY John Parker and
    Richard Rathbone
AFRICAN POLITICS Ian Taylor
AFRICAN RELIGIONS
    Jacob K. Olupona
AGEING Nancy A. Pachana
AGNOSTICISM Robin Le Poidevin
AGRICULTURE Paul Brassley and
    Richard Soffe
ALEXANDER THE GREAT
    Hugh Bowden
ALGEBRA Peter M. Higgins
AMERICAN BUSINESS HISTORY
    Walter A. Friedman
AMERICAN CULTURAL HISTORY
    Eric Avila
AMERICAN FOREIGN RELATIONS
    Andrew Preston
AMERICAN HISTORY Paul S. Boyer

AMERICAN IMMIGRATION
    David A. Gerber
AMERICAN INTELLECTUAL
    HISTORY
    Jennifer Ratner-Rosenhagen
THE AMERICAN JUDICIAL SYSTEM
    Charles L. Zelden
AMERICAN LEGAL HISTORY
    G. Edward White
AMERICAN MILITARY HISTORY
    Joseph T. Glatthaar
AMERICAN NAVAL HISTORY
    Craig L. Symonds
AMERICAN POETRY David Caplan
AMERICAN POLITICAL HISTORY
    Donald Critchlow
AMERICAN POLITICAL PARTIES
    AND ELECTIONS L. Sandy Maisel
AMERICAN POLITICS
    Richard M. Valelly
THE AMERICAN PRESIDENCY
    Charles O. Jones
THE AMERICAN REVOLUTION
    Robert J. Allison
AMERICAN SLAVERY
    Heather Andrea Williams
THE AMERICAN SOUTH
    Charles Reagan Wilson
THE AMERICAN WEST
    Stephen Aron
AMERICAN WOMEN'S HISTORY
    Susan Ware
AMPHIBIANS T. S. Kemp
ANAESTHESIA Aidan O'Donnell

WITTGENSTEIN A. C. Grayling
WORK Stephen Fineman
WORLD MUSIC Philip Bohlman
WORLD MYTHOLOGY David Leeming
THE WORLD TRADE
ORGANIZATION Amrita Narlikar

WORLD WAR II
Gerhard L. Weinberg
WRITING AND SCRIPT
Andrew Robinson
ZIONISM Michael Stanislawski
ÉMILE ZOLA Brian Nelson

Available soon:

IMAGINATION
Jennifer Gosetti-Ferencei

THE VICTORIANS
Martin Hewitt

For more information visit our website

www.oup.com/vsi/

Manfred B. Steger

GLOBALIZATION

A Very Short Introduction

SIXTH EDITION

OXFORD
UNIVERSITY PRESS

OXFORD

UNIVERSITY PRESS

Great Clarendon Street, Oxford, OX2 6DP,
United Kingdom

Oxford University Press is a department of the University of Oxford.
It furthers the University's objective of excellence in research, scholarship,
and education by publishing worldwide. Oxford is a registered trade mark of
Oxford University Press in the UK and in certain other countries

© Manfred B. Steger 2023

The moral rights of the author have been asserted

First edition published 2003
Second edition published 2009
Third edition published 2013
Fourth edition published 2017
Fifth edition published 2020

Published in the United States of America by Oxford University Press
198 Madison Avenue, New York, NY 10016, United States of America

British Library Cataloguing in Publication Data

Data available

Library of Congress Control Number: 2022951456

ISBN 978-0-19-288619-4

Printed and bound by
CPI Group (UK) Ltd, Croydon, CR0 4YY

In memory of Roland Robertson (1938–2022),
Model scholar, colleague, friend

Contents

Preface to the sixth edition

It is a gratifying experience to present readers with the sixth edition of a short book that has been so well received—not only in the English-speaking world, but around the world in more than 20 languages. The necessary task of updating and expanding this edition has been difficult in light of major global problems such as pandemics, soaring inflation, social inequality, climate change, cyber attacks, mass migrations, trade wars, job precarity, and the resurgence of nationalisms. Hence, it seems appropriate to refer to the present era as the 'Great Unsettling'—shorthand for the intensifying global dynamics of volatility, insecurity, and dislocation. Two recent events, in particular, have added to this disconcerting moment in human history.

First, starting in 2020, the COVID-19 pandemic swept across the world, uprooting the lives of its 7.8 billion inhabitants. By early 2023, official numbers showed that over 600 million people had contracted multiple variants of the disease, resulting in more than 7 million confirmed deaths. But the actual toll is likely much higher. Fortunately, effective vaccines were developed very quickly and by August 2022, more than 12 billion shots had been administered. For globalization scholars, this once-in-a-century health crisis proved to be an especially challenging research topic, since it required a multi-disciplinary approach to understanding the complexities involved in the spread and possible containment of the virus.

Second, Great Power competitions have been heating up in recent years. China, Russia, and India increasingly challenge US world leadership on multiple fronts. The Russian annexation of the Crimean Peninsula in 2014 and China's forward posture in the South China Sea, plus its political crackdown on Hong Kong, marked a new era of geopolitical conflict. Mounting tensions came to a head in 2022 with Russia's full-blown invasion of Ukraine. This major act of aggression was met with the imposition of unprecedented economic sanctions levied by a US-led broad coalition of countries against the Russian Federation. In response, President Putin vowed retaliation and escalated the war. For the first time since the end of the Cold War, a global nuclear confrontation appeared to be a distinct possibility.

Keeping such a complex topic as globalization brief and accessible in our era of the Great Unsettling becomes even more challenging in the case of a *very short* introduction. For this reason, the authors of the few existing introductions to the subject tend to concentrate on only one or two aspects of globalization—usually the emergence of the global economy, its history, structure, development, and supposed benefits and shortcomings. To be sure, a single-focus approach is helpful in explaining the impact and consequences of new techno-economic networks connecting people across borders and the transnational flows of goods, services, and labour. At the same time, however, such narrow accounts often leave the reader with a limited understanding of the full dimensions and complexity of globalization.

After all, the transformative powers of global interconnectedness reach deeply into *all* aspects of contemporary social life. Hence, the present volume makes the case that globalization also contains important *political, cultural, ecological,* and *ideological* aspects. Indeed, globalization occurs in people's heads as much as in the world 'out there'. Subjective globalization becomes visible in emotionally charged stories that describe and define that very process. The political forces behind these competing discourses resort to digitized media platforms to endow the buzzword with certain norms, values, and understandings. These not only legitimize and advance their specific power interests, but also shape the personal and collective identities of billions of people. Thus, it is mostly the *normative* question of whether globalization ought to be considered a 'good' or a 'bad' thing that has spawned heated debates in classrooms, boardrooms, and on the streets.

Some commentators applaud globalization for its proven ability to lift millions of people out of poverty, facilitate instant communication, and grant almost limitless access to information and Big Data. Nowhere has the success of globalization been more visible than in the impressive rise of the East Asian powerhouses China, Korea, and Japan. Other experts condemn globalization as a destructive force that annihilates traditional communal values, wrecks our planet, and stretches social disparities beyond sustainable levels. Regardless of which position is favoured, readers would be well advised to maintain a *critical* stance towards both interpretations.

To be sure, we should take comfort in the fact that the world is becoming a more interdependent place with the potential of enhancing ordinary people's lives. Boosting our mobility and connectivity across political borders and cultural divides represents an exciting development. We should also welcome sensible and compassionate policies that allow for the global flow of migrants and refugees. The same goes for technological progress—as long as it remains accountable to democratic citizens rather than reducing them to the status of digitally exploitable 'users'. Globalization should go hand in hand with the betterment of *all* people, especially those living in the disadvantaged regions of the global South. Most of all, securing sustainable forms of globalization demands that we take better care of our beautiful planet and all its sentient beings.

Let me end this Preface by recording my debts of gratitude. First, I want to thank my colleagues and students at the University of Hawai'i-Mānoa. Additional thanks are due to Paul James, professor of globalization and cultural diversity at the Institute for Culture and Society at Western Sydney University. I owe much to his steady intellectual encouragement and deep friendship. I appreciate the helpful feedback and support from numerous colleagues around the world who share my enthusiasm for the study of globalization. I want to express my sincere appreciation to numerous readers, reviewers, and audiences who, for nearly three decades, have made insightful comments in response to my public lectures and publications on globalization.

I appreciate Dr Tommaso Durante's competent research assistance on this edition as well as his formidable visual artist's eye for choosing some illustrations. Tommaso's pioneering 'Visual Archive Project of the Global Imaginary' can be found at: <https://www.the-visual-archive-project-of-the-global-imaginary. com/visual-global-imaginary>.

Luciana O'Flaherty and Jenny Nugee, my editors at Oxford University Press, have been shining examples of professionalism. Finally, a big thank you goes to my soul mate Perle Besserman—as well as the Steger, Besserman-Trigère, and Blanchette families—for their love and support. Many people have contributed to improving the quality of this book; its remaining flaws are my own responsibility.

List of illustrations

Globalization

List of maps

List of figures

List of tables

List of abbreviations

AI	Artificial Intelligence
APEC	Asian Pacific Economic Cooperation
ASEAN	Association of Southeast Asian Nations
BWR	Bretton Woods regime
BCE	Before the Common Era
CE	Common Era
CEO	chief executive officer
CFCs	chlorofluorocarbons
CITES	Convention on International Trade in Endangered Species of Wild Flora and Fauna
COVID-19	Coronavirus Disease 2019
ECB	European Central Bank
ESDC	European Sovereign Debt Crisis
EU	European Union
FDI	Foreign Direct Investment
G20	Group of Twenty
GATT	General Agreement on Tariffs and Trade
GDP	gross domestic product
GFC	Global Financial Crisis
GHGs	Global Greenhouse Gas Emissions
GJM	Global Justice Movement
GPS	Global Positioning System
ICT	information and communications technology
IMF	International Monetary Fund

INGO	international non-governmental organization
ISIL	Islamic State of Iraq and Levant
ISIS	Islamic State of Iraq and Syria
MERCOSUR	Mercado Común del Sur (Southern Common Market)
MSF/DWB	Médecins Sans Frontières/Doctors Without Borders
NAFTA	North American Free Trade Agreement
NASA	National Aeronautics and Space Administration
NATO	North Atlantic Treaty Organization
NGO	non-governmental organization
NYC	New York City
OAU	Organization of African Unity
OECD	Organization for Economic Cooperation and Development
OLED TV	Organic Light Emitting Diode Television
OPEC	Organization of Petroleum Exporting Countries
OWS	Occupy Wall Street
SAPs	Structural Adjustment Programmes
TNCs	transnational corporations
TPP	Trans-Pacific Partnership
UAE	United Arab Emirates
UK	United Kingdom
UN	United Nations
UNCTAD	United Nations Conference on Trade and Development
UNEP	United Nations Environment Programme
UNESCO	United Nations Educational, Scientific, and Cultural Organization
UNIPCC	United Nations Intergovernmental Panel on Climate Change
US	United States (of America)
WC	Washington Consensus
WEF	World Economic Forum
WHO	World Health Organization
WSF	World Social Forum

Chapter 1
What is globalization?

The earliest appearance of the term 'globalization' in the English language can be traced back to the 1930s. But it was not until the 1990s that the concept took the world by storm. The new buzzword captured the increasingly interconnected nature of social life on our planet and foregrounded the global integration of markets turbocharged by the ICT revolution. Three decades on, globalization has remained a hot topic. Today, one can track millions of references to the term in both virtual and printed spaces that range from enthusiastic embrace to blanket condemnation. In recent years, critical voices have become louder in the light of the nationalist resurgence around the world and the devastating COVID-19 pandemic that has disrupted seemingly indestructible global networks.

To make sense of these conflicting perspectives on globalization, let us start with matters of definition. Both the popular press and academic literature have been using 'globalization' in confusing ways to describe a process, a condition, a system, a force, or an age. Given that these concepts have very different meanings, a sloppy conflation of 'process' and 'condition' produces circular definitions that explain little. The often-repeated truism that globalization (the process?) leads to more globalization (the condition?) does not allow us to draw meaningful distinctions between causes and effects.

Key concepts: *globality*, *global imaginary*, *globalism*, *globalization*

To equip our definitional toolbox, let us distinguish between four different, but related, concepts. First, *globality* signifies a *social condition* characterized by tight global economic, political, cultural, and environmental interconnections and flows that challenge most of the currently existing borders and boundaries. Yet, we should not assume that globality is already upon us because it is an evolving condition. Nor does it suggest a fixed endpoint that precludes any further development. In fact, we could easily imagine different social manifestations of globality: one might be based primarily on values of individualism, competition, and deregulated capitalism, while another might draw on more communal arrangements, cooperative values, and the democratic regulation of economic arrangements.

Second, *global imaginary* refers to people's growing *consciousness* of the world as a single whole. This does not mean that nation and locality have lost their power to provide people with a sense of home and identity. But it would be a mistake to close one's eyes to the weakening of the national imaginary, as it was historically constructed in the 19th and 20th centuries. The intensification of global consciousness destabilizes and unsettles the nation-state framework within which people imagine their communal existence.

The rising global imaginary is linked to the rise of *globalisms*, our third concept. These new political ideologies articulate the overarching global imaginary into concrete policy agendas and political programmes. Globalisms spin stories about our increasingly interconnected world that serve particular power interests and contain value judgements about whether globalization should be considered a good or bad thing. We shall explore the various types of globalism in Chapter 7.

2

Our final, and most significant term, *globalization*, is a spatial concept referring to a *set of social processes* that is transforming our present social condition of conventional nationality into one of globality. Like 'modernization' and other verbal nouns that end in the suffix '-ization', the concept suggests a dynamic that evolves along discernible patterns but can also go into reverse at certain historical junctures. The root term 'global' indicates processes that operate at the transnational level such as the operation of global markets, worldwide investment flows, or the global dissemination of new styles of music such as Techno or K-Pop.

Yet another set of globalizing processes operates below the scale of the 'global'. In other words, globalization also takes place deep inside 'regional', 'national', and 'local' arenas. Rather than becoming irrelevant, these subglobal spaces get entangled with the global to produce multi-spatial forms of human contact. Globalization experts often refer to this complex interplay between the global and the local (and national) as *glocalization*. Think, for example, of major cities like Shanghai or Sydney that combine their specific urban environments with global standards for residential high-rise buildings, shopping malls, cultural events, and so on. Many people still have trouble recognizing that globalization affects all geographical scales ranging from the local to the global. Hence, it is crucial to bear in mind that globalization also manifests as glocalization.

Forms of globalization

These spatial complexities confirm that globalization should not be seen as a monolithic process. Rather, it is a set of dynamics that assumes four distinct, but interrelated, *social forms* (see Figure A).

The first social form, *embodied globalization*, manifests as the interconnectedness and mobility of *people* across our planet. As we shall discuss in Chapters 2 and 3, this is the oldest form of globalization and remains enduringly relevant in the

THE FOUR FORMS OF GLOBALIZATION
PEOPLE, IDEAS, THINGS, ORGANIZATIONS

(2) DISEMBODIED
IDEAS
(data, information, images)

(1) EMBODIED
PEOPLE
(tourists, refugees, business travellers)

GLOBALIZATION
Economic, political, cultural dynamics occur within and across all four forms

(3) OBJECTIFIED
THINGS
(tradable commodities, greenhouse gases, viruses)

(4) INSTITUTIONAL
ORGANIZATIONS (empires, states, military, corporations, churches, clubs)

A. Four forms of globalization.

contemporary movement of refugees, migrants, travellers, entrepreneurs, temporary workers, tourists, and so on. Concrete 21st-century examples include African political refugees crossing the Mediterranean into Europe and Central American migrants trying to trek across the Rio Grande valley into the United States in search of more sustainable lives. Privileged tourists can now complete intercontinental trips in mere hours in the comfort and security of a first-class aeroplane cabin. Only a century ago, the same journey would have taken several gruelling and dangerous weeks spent on a combination of ships, trains, motorcars, and horse- or oxen-drawn carriages.

The second form, *disembodied globalization*, is characterized by the worldwide interconnectedness and mobility of *ideas*, *data*, and *information*. As we shall observe in Chapters 2, 3, 5, 7, and 8, these include words, images, and electronic texts, and encoded capital such as blockchain enabled crypto-currencies like Bitcoin and Ethereum. This form has taken an enormous qualitative leap with the digital revolution, prompting commentators to speak of a 'new era of *digital globalization*'. There is little doubt that disembodied dynamics are emerging as the dominant form of globalization in the 21st century. Worldwide digitization has been greatly accelerated by the coronavirus-induced explosion of work and communication online.

The third form, *objectified globalization*, refers to the worldwide interconnectedness and mobility of *things* and *objects*. As discussed in Chapters 2, 3, 6, and 8, it includes tiny particles like GHGs and COVID-19 viruses, as well as large goods travelling on the ancient Silk Road from China to the Roman Empire or modern standardized shipping containers criss-crossing the world's oceans. Consider, for example, traded commodities such as a 'pre-loved' pair of Levi's jeans produced in the sweatshops of Bangladesh and destined for the coolest fashion temples of Milan; treasures of antiquity sold at skyrocketing prices at an international Internet auction in London; or your latest iPhone assembled and distributed via powerful global value chains. These contemporary manifestations of objectified globalization depend on digitally controlled delivery systems (such as amazon. com) that might offer AI-driven, drone-operated services in the near future.

The fourth form, *institutional globalization*, corresponds to the worldwide interconnectedness and mobility of *social* and *political institutions*. As discussed in Chapters 2, 3, 4, 5, and 8, it includes empires, states, TNCs, NGOs, churches, clubs, and so on. Its history can be traced back at least as far as the expansionist empires of Egypt, Persia, China, and Rome, and the proselytizing of the agents of Christendom and Islam more than a millennium ago. More recent examples include the half-million US military personnel stationed around the world; the global franchises of fast food enterprises like Subway or KFC; the hundreds of worldwide fan clubs of football favourites like Manchester United or Bayern Munich; and China's mind-boggling 'One Belt One Road' initiative—a monumental infrastructure project designed to extend Chinese economic and political influence across Asia, Africa, and Europe.

Qualities and dimensions of globalization

These four forms of globalization contain four distinct *qualities* or *characteristics*. First, they involve both the *creation* of new social networks and the *multiplication* of existing connections that cut across traditional political, economic, cultural, and geographical boundaries. For example, today's giant media corporations combine conventional TV coverage with multiple apps that feed into digital devices and social media sites that have long transcended nationally based services.

A second quality inherent in these four principal forms of globalization is the *expansion* or *stretching* of social relations, mobilities, and connections. Today's financial markets reach around the globe, and electronic trading occurs around the clock. Gigantic physical and virtual shopping malls cater to consumers who can afford commodities from all regions of the world—including products whose various components were manufactured in different countries and involve global supply chains.

Third, all forms of globalization also involve the *intensification* and *acceleration* of worldwide social interactions. As the Spanish sociologist Manuel Castells has pointed out, we have witnessed the creation of a *global network society* fuelled by what he calls *communication power*. This new form of power draws its strength from digital technological innovations that are reshaping the social landscape of human life.

Fourth, globalization does not merely unfold on an objective, material level but also involves the *subjective* plane of *human consciousness* and *imagination*. Without erasing local and national attachments, the *compression of space and time* has increasingly made the whole planet the frame of reference for human thought and action. In other words, globalization involves both the macro-structures of a global community and the micro-structures of global personhood. Mediated by digital technology largely controlled by large TNCs, the global extends deep into the core of the personal self, facilitating the creation of multiple and more fluid individual and collective identities.

All of these *forms* and *qualities* of globalization operate across the familiar social dimensions of everyday life: economics, politics, culture, ideology, and so on. However, given the increasing differentiation and specialization of knowledge creation, globalization dynamics tend to be analysed and explained in a rather one-dimensional manner. Dominated by economic perspectives on globalization, the debate over the relative importance of various domains has been raging for decades.

The ancient Buddhist parable of the blind scholars and their encounter with the elephant helps to illustrate the academic controversy over the significance of various dimensions of globalization. Since the blind scholars did not know what the elephant looked like, they resolved to obtain a mental picture, and thus the knowledge they desired, by touching the animal. Feeling its trunk, one blind man argued that the elephant was like a gigantic snake. Another man, rubbing along its enormous leg, likened the animal to a rough column of massive proportions. The third person took hold of its tail and insisted that the elephant resembled a large, flexible brush. The fourth man felt its sharp tusks and declared it to be like a great spear. Each of the blind scholars held firmly to his own idea of what constituted an elephant. Since their scholarly reputation was riding on the veracity of their respective findings, the blind men never ceased arguing over the true nature of the elephant (see Figure 1).

The academic quarrel over which dimension contains the essence of globalization represents a postmodern version of the parable of the blind men and the elephant. Scholars who equate globalization with a singular process clash with others over which aspect of social life constitutes its primary domain. Many experts

1. The globalization scholars and the elephant.

argue that economic processes lie at the core of globalization. Others privilege political, cultural, or ideological aspects. Still others point to environmental processes as being the essence of globalization. Like the blind men in the parable, each globalization researcher is partly right by correctly identifying *one* important dimension of the phenomenon in question. However, their collective mistake lies in their dogmatic attempts to reduce such a complex phenomenon as globalization to one or two domains that correspond to their own expertise.

The rise of Global Studies

To make matters even more complex, globalization is a geographically uneven set of processes that not only connect but sometimes also disrupt existing relations. Moreover, people living in various parts of the world are affected quite differently by today's gigantic compression of space and time. Unsurprisingly, then, scholars who approach the study of globalization from different academic fields not only hold different views with regard to primary dimensions of globalization, they also disagree on its scale, causation, chronology, impact, trajectories, and policy outcomes.

For this reason, they have raised myriad research questions that run in all directions. How does globalization proceed? What is driving it? Does it have one major dimension or is there a combination of equally significant domains? Is globalization a continuation of modernity or is it a radical break? Does it create new forms of inequality and hierarchy or offer new opportunities for poor and marginalized people? Notice that whenever researchers try to bring their object of enquiry into sharper focus, they also heighten the danger of provoking scholarly disagreements. Our subject is no exception.

One successful way of trying to improve the quality of communication among globalization researchers and develop a common framework has been the establishment of *Global Studies* starting in the 1990s. Although it has been extensively studied in traditional fields, globalization falls outside the established disciplinary framework. It is only of secondary concern in these conventional disciplines organized around different master concepts: 'society' in sociology; 'resources' and 'scarcity' in economics; 'culture' in anthropology; 'space' in geography; 'the past' in history; 'power' and 'governance' in political science, and so on. By contrast, global studies places 'globalization'—a contested keyword without a firm disciplinary home—at the core of its intellectual enterprise.

Today, Global Studies has emerged as a popular field of academic enquiry organized around four major conceptual pillars: globalization, transdisciplinarity, space and time, and critical thinking. Hundreds of Global Studies programmes have been established in universities on all continents. They invite millions of students to study globalization across traditional disciplinary boundaries in the social sciences, humanities, and even the natural sciences. The surging field covers vast literatures on related subjects that are usually studied in isolation from each other. The greatest challenge facing Global Studies lies, therefore, in bringing together the various strands of knowledge in ways that do justice to the fluidity and interdependencies of our fast-changing world.

International Relations versus Global Studies?

In the academic world, the term '*international* relations' (IR) refers to a subfield of Political Science dedicated to the systematic study of changing connections among territorial states and nationally bounded societies. Thus, IR scholars treated the nation-state as the main actor—and thus *the* central unit of analysis and the principal mover—of world politics. This framework is called *methodological nationalism* because it focuses on the self-interested actions of nation-states—especially with regard to security issues—and often at the expense of other crucial dimensions such as culture, ecology, and ideology. By contrast, Global Studies relies on *methodological globalism*. This framework treats transnational interconnections, mobilities, and imaginations as the basic units of analysis. Although Global Studies scholars acknowledge the enduring importance of states, they also emphasize the growing significance of non-state actors on the world stage such as NGOs, TNCs, churches, educational institutions, and other civil society organizations. Finally, Global Studies scholars also engage themes often neglected in IR, such as ecology, social space, media and communication, ideology, history, gender, race, ethnicity, technology, and poverty.

Our examination of the key concepts, forms, qualities, and dimensions of globalization—embedded in a new Global Studies academic framework—have prepared us to respond to the question that frames this chapter: 'What is globalization?' So let us attempt to formulate a *general definition* that satisfies experts and neophytes alike:

Globalization refers to the multidimensional and uneven expansion of social relations and consciousness across world-space and world-time.

Given the subtitle of our book, however, we ought to do better. So here is a *very short* definition of globalization in a mere eight words:

Globalization is about planetary interconnectivities, mobilities, and imaginations.

Chapter 2
Globalization in history

In this chapter, we consider an important objection raised by Global Studies scholars sensitive to historical matters: is globalization really a new phenomenon that is fundamentally different from the centuries-old process of modernization? Some critics have responded to this question in the negative, contending that even a cursory look at history suggests that there is not much that is new about contemporary globalization. Hence, before we explore in some detail the major dimensions of globalization, we should give this argument a fair hearing. After all, a critical investigation of globalization's alleged novelty and its relationship to modernity is closely related to yet another question hotly debated by globalization experts: what would a suitable historical chronology and periodization of globalization look like?

The definition of globalization we arrived at in Chapter 1 stresses its dynamic and multidimensional nature. In fact, the spatial expansion of social relations and the corresponding rise of the global imaginary are gradual processes with deep historical roots. The computer and software engineers who developed our mobile devices or the self-driving cars of the future stand on the shoulders of earlier innovators who created the steam engine, the cotton gin, the telegraph, the phonograph, the telephone, the typewriter, the internal-combustion engine, and electrical appliances. These products, in turn, owe their existence to much earlier technological inventions such as the telescope, the compass, water wheels, windmills, gunpowder, the printing press, and oceangoing ships.

And these innovations were the collective achievement of humans in all regions of the world, not just in one privileged geographic 'centre' called the 'West' or the 'North'. In order to acknowledge the full historical record of growing interdependence, we might reach back even further to such momentous technological and social achievements as the production of paper, the development of writing, the invention of the wheel, the domestication of wild plants and animals, the slow outward migration of our common African ancestors, and, finally, the emergence of language and the taming of fire at the dawn of human evolution.

Thus, the answer to the question of whether globalization is a 'new thing' depends upon how far we are willing to extend the web of causation that resulted in those recent technologies and social arrangements that most people have come to associate with our buzzword. Some Global Studies scholars consciously limit the historical scope of globalization to the post-1989 era in order to capture the uniqueness of its contemporary speed. Others are willing to extend this timeframe to include the ground-breaking developments of the last two centuries since the Industrial Revolution. Still others argue that globalization really represents the continuation and extension of complex processes that began with the emergence of modernity and the capitalist world system in the 1500s. But a few researchers refuse to confine globalization to time periods measured in mere decades or centuries. Rather, they suggest that these processes have been unfolding for millennia.

No doubt, each of these contending perspectives contains important insights. As we will see in this book, the advocates of the first approach have marshalled impressive evidence for their view that the dramatic expansion and acceleration of global exchanges since the 1980s represents a big leap in the history of globalization. The proponents of the second view correctly emphasize the tight connection between contemporary forms of globalization and the explosion of technology in the Industrial Revolution. The representatives of the third perspective rightly point to the significance of the time–space compression that occurred in the 16th century when Eurasia, Africa, and the Americas first became connected by enduring trade routes. Finally, the advocates of the fourth approach advance a rather sensible argument when they insist that any truly comprehensive account of globalization falls short without the incorporation of ancient developments and long-term dynamics into our planetary history.

While my short chronology of globalization that frames this chapter is necessarily fragmentary and general, it identifies five historical periods that are separated from each other by significant shifts in the pace of social exchanges as well as a widening of geographical scope. Thus, we could say that globalization is an ancient process that, over many centuries, has crossed distinct qualitative thresholds. Like a car transmission that accelerates the speed of the car, globalization has been shifting into higher gears while also going into reverse at times. Most importantly, my chronology rejects a Eurocentric perspective of world history. Involving all major regions and cultures of our planet, global history has unfolded in multidirectional flows originating from multiple civilizational centres. Moreover, the history of globalization is not a steady, linear ascent, but a constant up and down full of unanticipated surprises, violent twists, and sudden punctuations. Two such spectacular examples of dramatic reversals of growing worldwide interconnectivity include the fall of the Western Roman Empire in 476 CE (ushering the so-called 'dark ages' in Europe) and the nationalistic 20th-century interwar period (1918–39).

The prehistoric period (10,000 BCE–3500 BCE)

Let us begin roughly 12,000 years ago when small bands of
hunters and gatherers reached the southern tip of South America.
This event marked the end of the long process of settling all five
continents that was begun by our hominid African ancestors more
than one million years ago. Although some major island groups in
the Pacific and the Atlantic were not inhabited until relatively
recent times, the truly global dispersion of our species was finally
achieved. Completed by South American nomads, the success of
this endeavour rested on the migratory achievements of their
Siberian ancestors who had crossed the Bering Strait into North
America at least 1,000 years earlier.

Even in this earliest phase of globalization, contact among
thousands of hunter and gatherer bands occurred regularly.
But it remained geographically limited. This nomadic mode of
social interaction changed dramatically about 10,000 years ago
when humans took the crucial step of cultivating their own
crops. As a result of several factors, including the natural occurrence
of plants and animals suitable for domestication as well as
continental differences in area and total population size, only
certain regions located on or near the vast Eurasian landmass
proved to be ideal for these growing agricultural settlements.
These areas were located in the Fertile Crescent of the Middle
East, north-central China, North Africa, north-western India,
and New Guinea. Over time, food surpluses achieved by these
early farmers and herders led to population increases, the
establishment of permanent villages, and the construction of
fortified towns.

Over time, roving bands of nomads lost out to settled tribes,
chiefdoms, and, ultimately, to powerful states based on
agricultural food production (see Map 1). The decentralized,

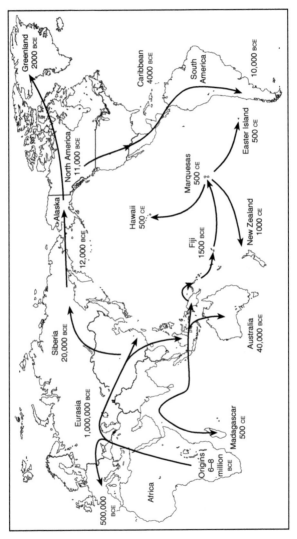

Map 1. Early human migration.

egalitarian nature of hunter and gatherer groups was replaced by centralized and highly stratified patriarchal social structures headed by chiefs and priests who were exempted from hard manual labour. Moreover, for the first time in human history, these farming societies were able to support two additional social classes whose members did not participate in food production. One group consisted of full-time craft specialists who directed their creative energies toward the invention of new technologies, such as powerful iron tools, beautiful ornaments made of precious metals, complex irrigation canals, sophisticated pottery and basketry, and monumental building structures. The other group, comprising professional priests, bureaucrats, and soldiers, played a key role in granting the monopolization of the means of violence to a few rulers; the precise accounting of food surpluses necessary for the growth and survival of the centralized state; the acquisition of new territory; the establishment of permanent trade routes; and the systematic exploration of distant regions.

For the most part, however, globalization in the prehistoric period was severely limited. Advanced forms of technology capable of overcoming existing geographical and social obstacles were largely absent. Thus, enduring long-distance interactions never materialized. It was only toward the end of this epoch that centrally administered forms of agriculture, religion, bureaucracy, and warfare slowly emerged as the key agents of intensifying modes of social exchange that would involve a growing number of societies in many regions of the world.

Perhaps the best way of characterizing the dynamic of this earliest phase of globalization would be to call it the *great divergence*—people and social connections stemming from a single origin but moving and diversifying greatly over time and across geographic space.

The premodern period (3500 BCE–1500 CE)

The invention of writing in Mesopotamia, Egypt, and central China between 3500 and 2000 BCE (see Figure 2) roughly coincided with the invention of the wheel around 3000 BCE in south-west Asia. Marking the close of the prehistoric period, these monumental inventions amounted to one of those technological and social boosts that shifted globalization into a higher gear. Thanks to the auspicious east–west orientation of Eurasia's major continental axis—a geographic feature that had already facilitated the rapid spread of crops and animals suitable for food production along the same latitudes—the diffusion of these new technologies to distant parts of the continent occurred within only a few centuries. The importance of these inventions for the strengthening of globalization processes should be obvious. Among other things, the wheel spurred crucial infrastructural innovations such as animal-drawn carts and permanent roads that allowed for the faster and more efficient transportation of people and goods. In addition to the spread of ideas and inventions, writing greatly facilitated the coordination of complex social activities and thus encouraged large state formations. Of the sizeable territorial units that arose during this period, only the Andes civilizations of South America managed to grow into the mighty Inca Empire without the benefits of either the wheel or the written word.

The later premodern period was the age of empires. As some states succeeded in establishing permanent rule over others, the resulting vast territorial accumulations formed the basis of the Egyptian kingdoms, the Persian Empire, the Macedonian Empire, the American empires of the Aztecs and the Incas, the Roman Empire, the Indian empires, the Byzantine Empire, the Islamic caliphates, the Holy Roman Empire, the African empires of Ghana, Mali, and Songhay, and the Ottoman Empire. All of these empires fostered the multiplication and extension of long-distance

2. Assyrian clay tablets with cuneiform writing, c.1900–1800 BCE.

communication and the exchange of culture, technology, commodities, and diseases. The most enduring and technologically advanced of these vast premodern conglomerates was undoubtedly the Chinese Empire. A closer look at its history reveals some of the early dynamics of globalization.

After centuries of warfare among several independent states, the Qin Emperor's armies, in 221 BCE, finally unified large portions of north-east China. For the next 1,700 years, successive dynasties known as the Han, Sui, T'ang, Yuan, and Ming ruled an empire supported by vast bureaucracies that would extend its influence to such distant regions as tropical South-East Asia, the Mediterranean, India, and East Africa (see Figure 3). Dazzling artistry and brilliant philosophical achievements stimulated new discoveries in other fields of knowledge such as astronomy, mathematics, and chemistry. The long list of major technological innovations achieved in China during the premodern period includes redesigned ploughshares, hydraulic engineering, gunpowder, the tapping of natural gas, the compass, mechanical clocks, paper, printing, lavishly embroidered silk fabrics, and sophisticated metalworking techniques. The construction of vast

3. The Great Wall of China.

irrigation systems consisting of hundreds of small canals enhanced the region's agricultural productivity while at the same time providing for one of the best river transport systems in the world. The codification of law and the fixing of weights, measures, and values of coinage fostered the expansion of trade and markets. The standardization of the size of cart axles and the roads they travelled on allowed Chinese merchants for the first time to make precise calculations as to the desired quantities of imported and exported goods.

The most spectacular of these trade routes was the Silk Road. It linked the Chinese and the Roman empires, with Parthian traders serving as skilled intermediaries, and reached the Italian peninsula in 50 BCE. Even 1,300 years later, a truly multicultural group of Eurasian and African globetrotters—including the famous Moroccan merchant and scholar Ibn Battuta and his Venetian counterparts in the Marco Polo family—relied on this great Eurasian land route to reach the splendid imperial court of the Mongol khans in Beijing. As noted in the Preface, China is currently working on the 21st-century renewal of the ancient Silk Road in the form of its massive One Belt One Road infrastructure project designed to connect Beijing to Western European cities.

By the 15th century CE, enormous Chinese fleets consisting of hundreds of 400-foot-long oceangoing ships were crossing the Indian Ocean and establishing short-lived trade outposts on the east coast of Africa. However, a few decades later, the rulers of the Chinese Empire implemented a series of fateful political decisions that halted overseas navigation and mandated a retreat from further technological development. This is another good example of the possible reversibility of globalization. The Chinese rulers cut short their empire's incipient industrial revolution, a development that allowed much smaller and less advanced European states to emerge as the primary historical agents behind the intensification of interconnectivity.

Toward the end of the premodern period, then, the existing global trade network (see Map 2) consisted of several interlocking trade circuits that connected the most populous regions of Eurasia and north-eastern Africa. Although both the Australian and the American continents still remained separate from this expanding web of economic, political, and cultural interdependence, the vast empires of the Aztecs and Incas had also succeeded in developing major trade networks in their own hemisphere.

The existence of these sprawling networks of economic and cultural exchange triggered massive waves of migration, which, in turn, led to further population increase and the rapid growth of urban centres. In the resulting cultural clashes, religions with only local significance were transformed into the major global religions we know today as Judaism, Christianity, Islam, Hinduism, and Buddhism. But higher population density and more intense social interaction over greater distances also facilitated the spread of new infectious diseases like the bubonic plague. An enormous

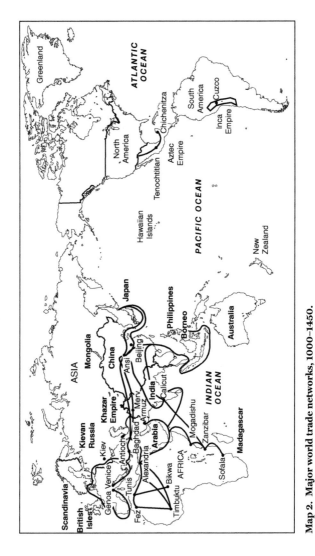

Map 2. Major world trade networks, 1000–1450.

epidemic of the mid-14th century, for example, killed up to one-third of the respective populations of China, the Middle East, and Europe. However, these unwelcome by-products of unfolding globalization processes did not reach their most horrific manifestation until the fateful 16th-century collision of the 'old' and 'new' worlds. Although the precise population size of the Americas before contact remains a contentious issue, it is estimated that the deadly germs of European invaders killed an estimated 18–20 million Native Americans—an inconceivable 90 to 95 per cent of the total indigenous population.

The early modern period (1500–1750)

The term 'modernity' has become associated with the 18th-century European Enlightenment project of developing science, achieving a universal form of morality and law, and liberating rational modes of thought and social organization from the perceived irrationalities of myth, religion, and political tyranny. But it is important to acknowledge the existence of multiple forms of modernity that evolved in various parts of the world in resistance to European modernity. The label 'early modern', then, refers to the period between the European Renaissance and the height of the Enlightenment. During these two centuries, Europe and its social practices emerged as the primary catalyst for globalization after a long period of Asian predominance.

Indeed, having contributed little to technology and other civilizational achievements between about 500 CE and 1000 CE, Europeans north of the Alps greatly benefited from the diffusion of technological innovations originating in the Islamic and Chinese cultural spheres. Despite the weakened political influence of China and the noticeable ecological decline of the Fertile Crescent some 500 years later, European powers failed to penetrate into the interior of Africa and Asia. Instead, they turned their expansionistic desires westward, searching for a new, profitable sea route to India and spreading the Christian religion.

Their efforts were aided by such innovations as mechanized printing, sophisticated wind- and water mills, extensive postal systems, revised maritime technologies, and advanced navigation techniques. Add the enormous impact of the Reformation and the related liberal political idea of limited government and popular sovereignty, and we have identified the main forces behind the qualitative leap that greatly intensified demographic, cultural, ecological, and economic flows between Europe, Africa, and the Americas.

Of course, the rise of European metropolitan centres and their affiliated merchant classes represented another important factor responsible for strengthening globalization tendencies during the early modern period. Embodying the new values of individualism and unlimited material accumulation, European economic entrepreneurs laid the foundation of what later scholars would call the 'capitalist world-system'. However, these fledgling merchant capitalists could not have achieved the global expansion of their commercial enterprises without substantial support from their respective governments. The monarchs of Spain, Portugal, the Netherlands, France, and England all put significant resources into the exploration of new worlds and the construction of new interregional markets that benefited them much more than their exotic 'trading partners'.

By the early 1600s, national joint stock companies like the Dutch and British East India companies were founded for the express purpose of setting up profitable overseas trade posts. As these innovative corporations grew in size and stature as a result of their exploitative and extractive practices, they acquired the power to regulate most intercontinental economic transactions, in the process implementing social institutions and cultural practices that enabled later colonial governments to place these foreign regions under direct political rule (see Figure 4). Related developments, such as the Atlantic slave trade and forced population transfers within the Americas, resulted in the

4. The sale of the island of Manhattan in 1626.

suffering and death of millions of non-Europeans while greatly benefiting white immigrants and their home countries.

To be sure, religious warfare within Europe also created its share of dislocation and displacement for Caucasian populations. Moreover, as a result of these protracted armed conflicts, military alliances and political arrangements underwent continuous modification. This highlights the crucial role of warfare as a catalyst of globalization. Evolving from the 1648 Westphalian peace treaty that ended the horrendous Thirty Years War that killed millions, the sovereign, territorial nation-state emerged in 18th-century Europe as the dominant framework of social life. As the early modern period drew to a close, contacts among nation-states were intensifying, creating both synergies and tensions.

The modern period (1750–1980s)

By the late 18th century, the great continent of Australia and the numerous Pacific islands were slowly incorporated into the European-dominated network of political, economic, and cultural exchange. Increasingly confronted with stories of 'distant lands' and images of exotic 'Others', Europeans and their migrant

25

descendants on other continents took it upon themselves to claim the role of the world's guardians of civilization and morality. In spite of their assumption of the moral high ground, however, the emerging middle classes perpetuated racist and sexist practices.

Creating the foundation for what would become the capitalist world-system, they also tolerated appalling levels of inequality both within their own societies and between the global North and South. Fed by a steady stream of materials and resources that originated mostly in other regions of the world, Western capitalist countries underwent an unprecedented 'Industrial Revolution'. Daring to resist powerful governmental controls, economic entrepreneurs and their academic counterparts like Adam Smith began to spread a philosophy of individualism and rational self-interest that glorified the virtues of an idealized capitalist system supposedly based upon the providential workings of the free market and its *invisible hand*.

But the 19th century also saw the first forms of working-class resistance to the exploitative practices of industrial capitalism. Written in 1847 by the German political radicals Karl Marx and Friedrich Engels, a passage taken from their famous *Communist Manifesto* captures the enormous qualitative shift in social relations that kicked globalization into a higher gear.

Indeed, the volume of world trade increased dramatically between 1850 and 1914. Guided by the activities of multinational banks, capital and goods flowed across the borders relatively freely as the sterling-based gold standard made possible the worldwide circulation of leading national currencies like the British pound and the Dutch guilder. Eager to acquire their own independent resource bases, most European nation-states subjected large portions of the global South to direct colonial rule. On the eve of the First World War during the so-called *belle époque* ('beautiful era'), merchandise trade measured as a percentage of gross

Marx and Engels on globalization

The discovery of America prepared the way for mighty industry and its creation of a truly global market. The latter greatly expanded trade, navigation, and communication by land. These developments, in turn, caused the further expansion of industry. The growth of industry, trade, navigation, and railroads also went hand in hand with the rise of the bourgeoisie and capital which pushed to the background the old social classes of the Middle Ages...Chased around the globe by its burning desire for ever-expanding markets for its products, the bourgeoisie has no choice but settle everywhere; cultivate everywhere; establish connections everywhere...Rapidly improving the instruments of production, the bourgeoisie utilizes the incessantly easing modes of communication to pull all nations into civilization—even the most barbarian ones...In a nutshell, it creates the world in its own image. (Translated by the author.)

national output totalled almost 12 per cent for the industrialized countries, a level unmatched until the 1970s. International pricing systems facilitated trade in important commodities like grains, cotton, and various metals. Brand name packaged goods like Coca-Cola drinks, Campbell soups, Singer sewing machines, and Remington typewriters made their first appearance. In order to raise the global visibility of these corporations, international advertising agencies launched the first full-blown transborder commercial promotion campaigns.

As Marx and Engels noted, however, the rise of the European bourgeoisie and the related intensification of global interconnections would not have been possible without the 19th-century explosion of science and technology. To be sure, the maintenance of these new industrial regimes required new energy sources such as electricity and petroleum. The largely unregulated use of these power sources resulted in the annihilation of countless animal and plant species as well as the toxification of entire regions. On the upside, however, railways, mechanized shipping, and 20th-century intercontinental air transport turbocharged embodied and objectified forms of globalization. Humanity was standing on the threshold of overcoming the last remaining geographical obstacles to the establishment of a genuine global infrastructure, while at the same time lowering transportation costs for goods and people alike.

These innovations in transportation were complemented by the swift development of communication technologies that served as the incubators of today's disembodied globalization. The telegraph and its transatlantic reach after 1866 provided for instant information exchanges between the two hemispheres. Moreover, the telegraph set the stage for the telephone and wireless radio communication, prompting newly emerging communication corporations like AT&T to coin advertising slogans in celebration of a world 'inextricably bound together'. Finally, the 20th-century arrival of mass circulation newspapers and magazines, film, and television further enhanced a growing consciousness of a rapidly shrinking world.

The modern period also witnessed an unprecedented population explosion. Having increased only modestly from about 300 million at the time of the birth of Christ to 760 million in 1750, the world's population reached 4.5 billion in 1980. Enormous waves of transcontinental migration intensified existing cultural exchanges and transformed traditional social patterns. Popular immigration countries like the United States of America, Canada, Australia, and New Zealand took advantage of this boost in human resources. By the early 20th century, America entered the world stage as a force to be reckoned with. At the same time, however, migration countries experienced major cultural backlashes steeped in racist attitudes, causing their governments to make significant efforts to control these large migratory flows. In the process, they invented novel forms of bureaucratic control and developed new surveillance techniques designed to accumulate more information about 'nationals' while keeping 'aliens' out.

When the accelerating process of industrialization sharpened existing disparities in wealth and wellbeing beyond bearable limits in the early 20th century, many working people in the global North began to organize themselves politically in various labour movements and socialist parties. However, their idealistic calls for international class solidarity went largely unheeded. Instead, ideologies that translated the national imaginary into radical political programmes captured the imagination of millions of people around the world. There is no question that interstate rivalries intensified in the 1930s as a result of the Great Depression, mass migration, urbanization, and industrial competition. This period of extreme nationalism culminated in the Second World War, genocides, and hostile measures to 'protect' narrowly conceived political communities that glorified cultural homogeneity.

The end of the Second World War saw the explosion of two powerful atomic bombs that killed more than 200,000 Japanese, most of them civilians. Nothing did more to convince people around the world of the impossibility of maintaining the illusion of geographically and politically separated 'nations'. A more positive result was the accelerating process of decolonization in the 1950s and 1960s that created new nation-states in the global South while at the same time intensifying global flows and international exchanges. A new political order of sovereign but interdependent nation-states anchored in the charter of the United Nations raised the prospect of global democratic governance. However, such internationalist hopes quickly faded as the Cold War divided the world for four long decades into two antagonistic spheres: a liberal-capitalist *First World* dominated by the United States, and an authoritarian-communist *Second World* controlled by the Soviet Union. Both 'blocs' sought to establish their political and ideological dominance in what came to be known as the *Third World*.

Clearly this tripartite division of geography in terms of 'worlds' attests to the rise of a global imaginary. Thus, the idea of 'global' was not necessarily associated with positive meanings. After all, superpower confrontations like the 1962 Cuban Missile Crisis raised the spectre of a global conflict capable of destroying virtually all life on our planet. Indeed, this horrific moment of the world at the brink of annihilation found its permanent expression in the Cold War acronym MAD ('mutually assured destruction').

During the 1960s and 1970s two significant developments, in particular, facilitated the rise of the global imaginary. The first was the advent of space travel, an achievement best captured in pictorial form in the stunning images of 'Earthrise' (see Figure 5).

5. Earthrise.

Snapped in 1968 by Apollo 8 astronaut William Anders during the first-ever manned orbit of the moon, this photo reveals the haunting fragility of our tiny blue-white marble suspended in the vast expanse of the universe. Reaching a global audience almost instantaneously, the photos did much to enhance people's awareness of their collective journey on 'Spaceship Earth'. For the first time in history, people blessed with access to televisions or illustrated magazines could see their home planet through the eyes of the Greek god Apollo whose name adorned the US space mission. These extraordinary images of our 'global village' also demonstrated the crucial role of visuality and emotions in stimulating human imagination of the world as a whole.

This meant that, second, human sentiments of belonging were now mediated through planetary images. The significance of planetary visuality was reinforced by new ecological perspectives such as James Lovelock's influential GAIA model. The British scientist working for NASA presented a compelling theory of Earth as a single superorganism functioning as a self-regulating global system. Such holistic perspectives contributed to the forging of transnational environmental movements and the creation of a global 'Earth Day'. Images of our fragile planet suddenly appeared on T-shirts, tote bags, and coffee mugs. Counterculture magazines of the 1960s like the popular *Whole Earth Catalog* projected the importance of ecological issues across national borders. Unsurprisingly, it was during these opening decades of the space age and environmentalism that the academic and popular use of the word 'global' skyrocketed.

The contemporary period (from the 1980s)

As we noted at the beginning of this chapter, the dramatic creation, expansion, and acceleration of worldwide interconnectivities and global consciousness that has occurred since the 1980s represents yet another quantum leap in the history of globalization. The best way of characterizing this latest globalization wave would be to call it *the great convergence*—different and widely spaced people and social connections coming together more rapidly than ever before. This dynamic received another boost with the 1991 collapse of the communist Soviet bloc and 'neoliberal' attempts to create an integrated global market.

As we explore in Chapter 3, the deregulation of national economies turbocharged a new phase of globalization. The unprecedented development of horizontal networks of digital communication connecting the local and global was made possible through the worldwide diffusion of the Internet, wireless communication, and digital social media. And forays into outer space accelerated. The big story became the commercialization of space. According to the Union of Concerned Scientists, between 1991 and 2000 there were 118 satellite launches—80 per cent of which were commercial and the remainder governmental or military. In 2018 alone, 372 satellites were launched, more than 20 times the level at the turn of the century. But even manned space travel continued with the expansion of the international space station and the proliferation of private space exploration ventures such as billionaires Richard Branson's *Virgin Galactic*, Elon Musk's *SpaceX*, and Jeff Bezos's *Blue Origin*.

But how, exactly, has globalization accelerated in these last three decades? What dimensions of social activity have been most affected by globalization? Is contemporary globalization a 'good' or a 'bad' thing? Are the proliferation of populist movements and the explosion of the COVID-19 virus upon an unsuspecting world ominous signs that we are entering a phase of 'deglobalization'?

In the remaining chapters of this book, our exploration of the major dimensions of globalization will suggest possible answers to these crucial questions. In doing so, we will limit the application of the term 'globalization' to the contemporary period while keeping in mind the main lesson of this chapter: the forces driving it can be traced back thousands of years.

Moreover, let us recall that globalization is a multidimensional set of processes whose four major forms operate simultaneously and unevenly across all geographical scales. One could compare these overlaps and interactions to the intricately connected parts of a roaring Ferrari V-12 engine. Just as an apprentice car mechanic must turn off and disassemble this precious car engine in order to understand its operation, so must students of globalization switch off the complexity of the real-world flows and apply analytical distinctions in order to make sense of the massive assemblage of global interconnectivity. Hence, the ensuing chapters examine the various domains of globalization in isolation while resisting the temptation to reduce it to a single 'most important' aspect. Only in this way can we hope to avoid the blunder that kept the blind men from appreciating the elephant in its full glory.

Chapter 3
The economic and technological dimensions of globalization

If we asked ordinary persons on the busy streets of global cities like New York, London, Shanghai, São Paulo, or Melbourne about the essence of globalization, their answers would probably involve some reference to growing forms of economic connectivity fuelled by digital technologies. Thus, they might point to their mobile devices such as Cloud-connected smart wireless phones like the Android or sleek digital tablets like the iPad, linked to powerful Internet browsers like Google Chrome that sort in a split second through gigantic data sets. Or they might mention the burgeoning video-postings on YouTube or TikTok; digital social networking sites like Meta and Twitter; the blogosphere; Cloud-based voice services like Amazon's Alexa; satellite- and computer-connected OLED TVs, Netflix movie streaming; 3D printing, immersive video games; a new generation of voice-activated GPS and navigation units to be installed in self-driving electric cars of the future; and the proliferation of globally recognizable QR codes. Indeed, these ubiquitous matrix barcodes are utilized by billions of individuals and businesses to store commercial information as well as to advertise products, services, and events globally.

Economic globalization refers to the intensification and stretching of economic connections across the globe. Gigantic flows of capital

Techno-economic globalization in action: the magic of QR codes

'QR' stands for 'quick response' and refers to those square-shaped, black-and-white barcodes made up of hundreds of shapes of 'bits' that nowadays adorn most economic products and advertisements. By using a cell phone and a QR reader app, scanning a QR code might yield the price of the product, make a payment, track a shipment, identify documents, display a text, connect to a wireless network, or open a webpage in the cell phone's browser. Or it might yield a globally accessible website advertising the local event. Invented in 1994 by the Japanese company Denso Wave to track vehicles, the largest QR codes can store up to 15,000 bits that can be arranged in 2.81796087 $9631397637428637785383222308241674912977296 \times 10^{4515}$ different ways. This number is larger than all traceable items on Earth combined.

mediated by digital technology and standardized means of transportation have stimulated trade in goods and services. Extending their reach around the world, markets have migrated to cyberspace and integrated local, national, and regional economies. Huge transnational corporations (TNCs), powerful international economic institutions, and gigantic regional business and trade networks like the Asian Pacific Economic Cooperation (APEC), the Association of Southeast Asian Nations (ASEAN), the Southern Common Market (MERCOSUR), and the European Union (EU) have emerged as the major regional building blocks of the 21st century's global economic order.

It is difficult to disentangle any discussion of economic globalization from its technological aspects. In fact, technology is not external to other forces that shape our lives but combines with economic, political, and cultural dynamics in powerful ways.

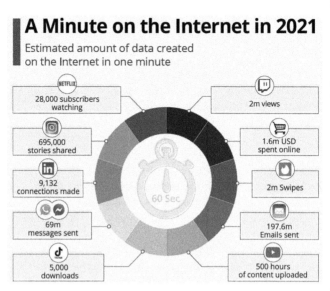

A Minute on the Internet in 2021

Estimated amount of data created
on the Internet in one minute

NETFLIX
28,000 subscribers
watching

2m views

695,000
stories shared

1.6m USD
spent online

9,132
connections made

2m Swipes

69m
messages sent

197.6m
Emails sent

5,000
downloads

500 hours
of content uploaded

60 Sec

B. A minute on the Internet in 2021.

Recent advances in digital technology, in particular, have played a
crucial role in profound social transformations centred on the
market. The Internet (see Figure B), in particular, assumes a
pivotal function in the expanding glocal networks that involve all
dimensions of globalization. After all, the World Wide Web
connects individuals, millions of civil society associations, and
thousands of state and local governments around the world. In
2022, more than 5 billion people around the world utilized
the Internet.

Let us start our exploratory journey into economic globalization
with a concrete example that highlights how digital technology is
transforming business and society. Consider the amazing, yet true,
story of a young American journalist whose loss of his cell phone
brought him celebrity status and economic success in China and
across the planet.

How a stolen iPhone made the career of a young journalist

After a Happy Hour wine binge in a NYC East Village bar in February 2014, Matt Stopera noticed that his iPhone was missing. For the young American journalist working for BuzzFeed—a US-based Internet news and entertainment company with a focus on digital media—the loss of his cell phone was almost tantamount to losing his eyesight. After recovering from his initial shock, Matt did what the millions of global victims of cell phone theft tend to do: he got a new one and tried to forget the frustrating experience as quickly as possible. Most cell phone theft stories end here. But Matt's didn't.

A year later, he was sitting in his small NYC flat browsing through his private photo stream on his new cell phone when he came across a slew of pictures he had not taken. They included more than 20 images of a young Asian man standing in front of an orange tree. For over a month, daily updates of the 'orange man' pictures kept popping up. Trying to solve the mystery, he consulted with an Apple employee who speculated that the pictures had been taken somewhere in China. That's where most stolen cell phones end up—millions each year. The Apple genius also revealed the reason for the appearance of these alien pictures: his current phone and the stolen one still shared the same iCloud account. Matt immediately deleted everything on his phone and asked for his former device to be deactivated. Confident that these actions would put an end to the hassle, he left the store.

On second thought, however, Matt decided to get to the bottom of the mystery. He created the following post on BuzzFeed: *Who is this man and why are his pictures showing up on my phone?* Within hours, he received numerous tweets from Chinese people offering him help in finding 'orange man'. But how could there be such a swift and massive response from hundreds of tweeters thousands of miles away? Well, a famous user of Sina Weibo—a Chinese micro-blogging website and leading social media platform with nearly 600 million monthly active users—had cross-posted his BuzzFeed post, thus triggering the virtual hunt for the mystery 'orange man' that soon went viral. Told that he had become an overnight Internet celebrity in China, Matt followed the advice of his new virtual fans and joined Weibo. The next day, he had 50,000 followers. Within a week, the number climbed to 160,000. Soon thereafter, he reached 1,000,000.

By that time, the mystery man, Li Hongjun, had been found in the south-east coastal province of Guandong. Paying close attention to this viral explosion, Weibo gave Li the nickname 'Brother Orange' and encouraged the two men to meet in China. Within days, the story skyrocketed to the top of Weibo's trending topics as 60 million users were following along to see if and when the pair would meet. Many of them began signing up for US-based social networking platforms like Facebook and Twitter, even though these sites were technically banned in China. Matt also responded to lucrative requests from some Chinese fans to start teaching them English using video posts. His tutoring venture became a commercial success, and he received the Chinese nickname 'Doubi', which translates loosely as 'Mr Bean'. At this point, 'Doubi' and 'Bro' Orange' had been exchanging electronic messages on a daily basis. Their interactions revealed that Bro' Orange was a married man with four children and owned a successful restaurant called Jade Tea Farm in Meizhou, a thriving city of 4.3 million.

In March 2015, their highly anticipated meeting took place. On Matt's three-legged plane flight from NYC to Guandong, he was recognized by several Chinese passengers. Upon landing at Meizhou airport, he was mobbed by droves of fans who had queued up for hours to welcome their American idol. As Matt put it, 'Basically, I now know what it feels like to be Kim K at LAX with Kanye and Northwest.' Wildly cheering the first hug between the two long-distance iPhoto pals, the fans also applauded the return of the stolen iPhone to its original owner. It turned out that Li was entirely innocent, having received the phone as a gift from a distant relative.

Talking through translators, and sponsored by Weibo, the pair embarked on a triumphant publicity tour through Li's home province. Travelling in a comfortable bus and two special cars that featured big decals of their faces, their journey was heavily documented on social media. Followed every minute by a large press contingent demanding constant interviews, the pair interacted with numerous local fans, who held up gigantic welcome signs and were eager to take selfies with their heroes. The pair's week-long journey ended with a memorable Weibo-sponsored trip to Beijing, where they visited famous landmarks like Tiananmen Square (Figure 6).

6. BuzzFeed writer Matt 'Doubi' Stopera and Li 'Brother Orange' Hongjun visit Beijing's Tiananmen Square.

After Matt's trip to China, Li returned the favour and paid a highly advertised visit to his American pal. Matt showed off his NYC home turf and also took his Bro' to Las Vegas. Unexpectedly, the celebrity pair was invited to NBC's Emmy Award-winning *The Ellen DeGeneres Show*. Enjoying their superstar status, the pair also attended a Britney Spears concert where they met the pop diva in a private session and took loads of pictures that delighted the fans back in China.

Eventually, the astonishing tale of how a stolen iPhone ended up in China was shared internationally on social media more than 100 million times. Not only did it make for fantastic entertainment, but, more importantly, it yields important insights into the intertwined dynamics of economic and technological globalization. First, the tale demonstrates that these two domains should not be seen as separate spheres. Rather, they constitute interrelated nodes of expanding and intensifying social interdependencies.

Second, the story points to a remarkable feature of today's global economy: the growing earning potential of creative entrepreneurs equipped with cutting-edge technology. Matt's oversized digital footprint resulted not only in lucrative language and entertainment gigs, but it also opened the door to Hollywood. *Brother Orange*, a major feature film based on the tale of the lost iPhone, entered development in 2016 and is intended for global distribution. The big-screen venture unites four production companies around the world under the commercial umbrella of a transnational enterprise called 'Flagship Entertainment': American-based Warner Brothers and BuzzFeed Studios, China-based China Media Capital, and Hong Kong-based broadcaster TVB. This film deal also prompted Matt to create his own 'start-up' entertainment business and thus join thousands of other young entrepreneurs in pursuit of their global digital dreams. Indeed, more than $288 billion in venture capital was invested worldwide in new start-ups in 2020—a 15 per cent annual growth rate since 2001.

No doubt, Matt's story shows that the smartphone is a transformative social force of planetary proportions. It also proved the intuitions of ordinary persons on the streets right: economics and technology are intertwined drivers of globalization. Technology is remaking economics and economics is shaping technology. But why and how did economic connections across the globe take off and intensify so quickly over the last few decades?

The emergence of the global economic order

Contemporary economic globalization can be traced back to the emergence of a new international economic order assembled at a watershed economic conference held towards the end of the Second World War in the sleepy New England town of Bretton Woods (see Figure 7). Under the leadership of the United States and Great Britain, the major powers of the global North agreed to reverse their protectionist policies of the interwar period. In addition to arriving at a firm commitment to expand trade, the participants of the conference also established binding rules on international economic activities. Moreover, they resolved to create a more stable monetary exchange system in which the value of each country's currency was pegged to a fixed gold value of the US dollar. Within these prescribed limits, however, individual nations were free to control the permeability of their borders.

The Bretton Woods regime (BWR) also established three new international economic organizations. The International Monetary Fund (IMF) was created to administer the international monetary system. The International Bank for Reconstruction and Development, later known as the World Bank, was initially designed to provide loans for Europe's postwar reconstruction. During the 1950s, however, its purpose was expanded to fund various industrial projects in developing countries around the world. Finally, the General Agreement on Tariffs and Trade (GATT) was established in 1947 as a global trade organization charged with

7. The 1944 Bretton Woods Conference.

fashioning and enforcing multilateral trade agreements. In 1995, the World Trade Organization (WTO) was founded as the successor organization to GATT. By the turn of the century, the WTO had become the focal point of intense public controversy over the design and the effects of economic globalization.

In operation for almost three decades, the BWR contributed greatly to the establishment of what some observers have called the 'golden age of controlled capitalism' (1945–80). Trade and foreign direct investment (FDI) expanded faster than the world GDP and the share of exports in global output tripled from less than 5 per cent in 1945 to 16 per cent in 1981. Even conservative political parties in Europe and the United States embraced some version of state interventionism proposed by the celebrated British economist John Maynard Keynes, one of the chief architects of the BWR. A wage compromise between big business and labour together with strong mechanisms of state control over international capital movements made possible full employment and the expansion of the welfare state in the prosperous countries of the global North. Rising wages and increased social services secured a temporary class compromise that facilitated the expansion of the middle class.

In 1971, however, the BWR took a severe blow when US President Richard Nixon abandoned the gold standard—the long-term basis for setting the rules of economic management based on stable rates of currency exchange—in response to profound political changes in the world that were undermining the economic competitiveness of American industries. By the end of the decade, the industrialized world was hit by a toxic combination of factors known as 'stagflation': high inflation, low economic growth, high unemployment, public sector deficits, and two unprecedented

Neoliberalism

Neoliberalism is rooted in the classical liberal ideals of Adam Smith (1723–90) and David Ricardo (1772–1823). These British thinkers viewed the market as a self-regulating mechanism tending towards equilibrium of supply and demand, thus securing the most efficient allocation of resources. They argued that any constraint on free competition would interfere with the efficiency of market mechanisms, inevitably leading to social stagnation, political corruption, and the creation of unresponsive state bureaucracies. They also advocated the elimination of tariffs on imports and other barriers to trade and capital flows between nations. British sociologist Herbert Spencer (1820–1903) added to this doctrine a twist of 'social Darwinism' by boasting that free market economies constitute the most civilized form of human competition in which the 'fittest' would naturally rise to the top.

energy crises due to the Organization of Petroleum Exporting Countries (OPEC)'s ability to control a large part of the world's oil supply. Progressive political forces in the global North most closely identified with the model of controlled capitalism suffered a series of spectacular election defeats at the hands of conservative political parties that advocated what came to be called a 'neoliberal' approach to economic and social policy.

In the 1980s, British Prime Minister Margaret Thatcher and US President Ronald Reagan led this *neoliberal revolution* against Keynesian principles of government regulation. Neoliberals asserted that releasing private economic activity from state control would provide a tremendous lift to world trade, investment, and living standards. To boost the legitimacy of their new ideas, pro-business elites in the global North consciously linked the novel term 'globalization' to a political agenda aimed at the 'liberation' and deregulation of state-regulated economies around the world. Neoliberalism quickly globalized and received further legitimization with the 1989–91 collapse of Soviet communism.

Concrete neoliberal measures

1. Privatization of public enterprises.
2. Deregulation of the economy.
3. Liberalization of trade and industry.
4. Massive tax cuts.
5. 'Monetarist' measures to keep inflation in check, even at the risk of increasing unemployment.
6. Strict control on organized labour.
7. The reduction of public expenditures, particularly social spending.
8. The downsizing of government.
9. The expansion of international markets.
10. The removal of controls on global financial flows.

Since then, the three most significant dynamics related the neoliberal acceleration of economic globalization have been the internationalization of trade and finance, the increasing power of transnational corporations and large investment banks, and the role of international economic institutions like the IMF, the World Bank, and the WTO. In the remainder of this chapter, we will examine these important features of economic globalization as well as some of the challenges that have subsequently emerged.

The internationalization of trade

Many people associate economic globalization with the controversial issue of free trade. After all, the total value of world trade exploded from $57 billion in 1947 to an astonishing record high $28.5 trillion in 2021. This apex was reached despite the severe short-term economic shock of the COVID-19 pandemic (discussed below). Dramatic advances in shipping container technology proved to be one of the key factors in the globalization of trade. Once the standardization of shipping containers was agreed to in 1965, the 8 feet wide, 8½ feet high, and 10, 20, or 40-foot-long boxes could be handled by ports around the world and rolled straight onto flat-bed trucks. The first ships holding such standardized containers could only hold about 200 boxes. But staggering advances in the ship-building industry and related digital technologies produced in 2020 the world's largest container ship, the HMM *Algeciras*, which was capable of holding nearly 24,000 of these large boxes (see Figure 8). Moreover, the dramatic decline in sea-freight costs until COVID-19 hit led to a tripling of container port traffic in the first two decades of the 21st century.

However, the electoral success of pro-trade tariff nationalists like Donald Trump, Boris Johnson, and Marine Le Pen demonstrates that the public debate over the alleged benefits and drawbacks of free trade has been taking a negative turn over the last decade. Wealthy pro-market Northern governments and regional trading blocs can no longer rely on public opinion and political support in

8. HMM *Algeciras*—the biggest container ship in the world (2020).

their efforts to establish a single global market. For example, in 2017, the protectionist Trump administration withdrew from the Trans-Pacific Partnership (TPP). This far-reaching pact would have established the largest free-trade trading bloc in the world. The remaining 11 countries—including China, Canada, and Australia—managed to salvage only a revised, downsized version of the treaty.

Still, a dwindling number of pro-free trade governments have held fast to the original neoliberal promise that the elimination or reduction of existing trade barriers among nations would increase global wealth and enhance consumer choice. The ultimate benefit of integrated markets, they argue, would be secure peaceful international relations and technological innovation for the benefit of all. There is, indeed, evidence that some national economies have increased their productivity as a result of free trade. Millions of people have been lifted out of poverty in developing countries such as China, India, Vietnam, and Indonesia. As the last available World Bank data show, the percentage of people living in extreme poverty (on less than $1.90

a day) fell from nearly 50 per cent in 1990 to an astonishing 9.2 per cent in 2019. Moreover, there are some clear material benefits that accrue to societies through economic specialization, competition, and digitization.

On the flipside, however, the UN has announced that its target of reducing the number of people living in poverty to less than 250 million by 2030 will not be met. In addition, inequalities in income and wealth have skyrocketed, especially *within* nations, suggesting that the benefits of neoliberal globalization accrue disproportionally at the top. Empirical data demonstrate that profits resulting from free trade have not been distributed fairly within and among various income groups. According to a 2021 Economic Policy Institute report, chief executives of America's top 350 companies earned 351 times more than the average worker in 2020. In 1965, the ratio of CEO to worker pay stood at only 20:1.

The distribution of global wealth also shows that only a few countries possess most assets. The entire African continent captures less than 1 per cent of the world's wealth. As a 2022 Oxfam report shows, the world's 10 richest billionaires—most of them residing in the global North—own more assets than the bottom 40 per cent of humanity or 3.1 billion people. While the number of billionaires has more than doubled between 2008 and 2020, the share of tax revenues paid by large corporations has dropped significantly.

The unleashing of global financial flows

The internationalization of trade has gone hand in hand with the liberalization of global financial flows. Its key components include the deregulation of interest rates, the removal of credit controls, the privatization of government-owned banks and financial institutions, and the explosive growth of investment banking. Globalization of financial trading allows for increased mobility among different segments of the financial industry, with fewer restrictions and greater investment opportunities. Cutting-edge satellite systems and fibre-optic cables provided the nervous system of Internet-based technologies that further accelerated the liberalization of financial transactions. As captured by the snazzy title of Bill Gates's best-selling book at the turn of the 21st century, *business@the-speed-of-thought* has become commonplace today. Millions of individual and institutional investors utilize global real-time electronic investment networks not only to place their orders at the world's leading stock exchanges, but also to receive instant information about relevant developments.

But a large part of the money involved in this *financialization of global capitalism* that swept the first decade of the new century had little to do with supplying capital for such productive investments as assembling machines or organizing raw materials and employees to produce saleable commodities. Most of the financial growth came from increases in lending in the property sector, often in the form of *high-risk hedge funds* and other purely money-dealing currency and securities markets, which seek profits from future production. In other words, investors were betting on commodities or currency rates that did not yet exist. Dominated by highly sensitive stock markets that drive high-risk innovation, the world's financial systems became characterized by high volatility, brutal competition, general insecurity, and even outright fraud. Global speculators often took advantage of weak financial and banking regulations to make astronomical profits in the emerging markets of developing countries. However, since these international capital flows can be reversed swiftly, they are capable of creating artificial boom-and-bust cycles that endanger the social welfare of entire regions. This is precisely what triggered the 1997–8 *Asian Economic Crisis* that caused havoc in the region.

In 2008, the volatility of financial flows unleashed by three decades of neoliberal deregulation culminated in a global meltdown, followed by an ongoing period of chronic economic instability. Thus, before we continue our exploration of economic globalization with respect to the increasing power of TNCs and the enhanced role of international economic institutions, let us pause for a moment to examine briefly the two suspects most responsible for our current era of global economic instability and volatility: the 2008 *Global Financial Crisis* (GFC) leading to the European Sovereign Debt Crisis (ESDC); and the economic shocks caused by the *COVID-19 pandemic* of the early 2020s.

The era of global economic instability: from the GFC to the COVID-19 pandemic

The GFC has its roots in the 1980s and 1990s, when three successive US governments under Presidents Reagan, Bush I, and Clinton pushed for the significant deregulation of the domestic financial services industry. The neoliberal deregulation of US finance capital resulted in a frenzy of mergers that gave birth to huge financial-services conglomerates eager to plunge into securities ventures in areas that were not necessarily part of their underlying business. *Derivatives, financial futures, credit default swaps*, and other esoteric financial instruments became extremely popular when new computer-based mathematical models suggested more secure ways of managing the risk involved in buying an asset in the future at a price agreed to in the present. Relying far less on savings deposits, financial institutions borrowed from each other and sold these loans as securities, thus passing the risk on to investors in these securities. Other 'innovative' financial instruments, such as hedge funds leveraged with borrowed funds, fuelled a variety of speculative activities. Billions of investment dollars flowed into complex 'residential mortgage-backed securities' that promised investors up to a 25 per cent return on equity.

Assured by monetarist policies of the US Federal Reserve Bank aimed at keeping interest rates low and credit flowing abundantly, investment banks around the world eventually expanded their search for capital by buying risky *subprime loans* from mortgage brokers who, lured by the promise of big commissions, were accepting applications for housing mortgages with little or no down payment and without credit checks. Investment banks snapped up these high-risk loans knowing that they could resell these assets—and thus the risk involved—by bundling them into composite securities no longer subject to government regulation. Indeed, one of the most complex of these 'innovative' instruments of securitization—so-called *collateralized debt obligations*—often hid the problematic loans by bundling them together with lower-risk assets and reselling them to unsuspecting investors. Moreover, they were backed by positive credit ratings reports issued by credit ratings giants like Standard and Poor's and Moody's. The high yields flowing from these new securities funds attracted more and more investors around the world, thus rapidly globalizing more than US$1 trillion worth of what came to be known as *toxic assets*.

In mid-2007, however, the financial steamroller finally ran out of fuel when seriously overvalued American real estate began to drop and foreclosures shot up dramatically. Some of the largest and most venerable financial institutions, insurance companies, and government-sponsored underwriters of mortgages such as Lehman Brothers, Bear Stearns, Merrill Lynch, Goldman Sachs, AIG, Citicorp, J. P. Morgan Chase, IndyMac Bank, Morgan Stanley, Fannie Mae, and Freddie Mac—to name but a few—either

Money and the GFC: what do these numbers mean?

When reading about the GFC, huge numbers are splashed around very liberally. In spite of their similar spellings, million, billion, and trillion represent radically different orders of magnitude. Consider this hypothetical situation: if you spent US$1 every second, you would spend US$1 million in about 12 days. At the same rate, it would take you approximately 32 years to spend US$1 billion. Taking this to the next level, US$1 trillion would take you 31,546 years to spend!

declared bankruptcy or had to be bailed out by the US taxpayers at the tune of hundreds of billions of dollars.

But one of the major consequences of the failing financial system was that banks trying to rebuild their capital base could hardly afford to keep lending large amounts of money. The flow of global credit froze to a trickle and businesses and individuals who relied on credit found it much more difficult to obtain. This credit shortage, in turn, impacted the profitability of many businesses, forcing them to cut back production and lay off workers. Industrial output declined, and unemployment shot up, as the world's stock markets dropped dramatically.

By 2009, the GFC had turned into what came to be known as the *Great Recession*; $14.3 trillion, or 33 per cent of the value of the world's companies, had been wiped out. The developing world was especially hard hit by the declining demand for their exports. The leaders of the group of the world's 20 largest economies (G20) met repeatedly in the early 2010s to devise a common strategy to forestall a global depression (see Map 3).

Although most countries eventually pulled out of the Great Recession, economic growth in many parts of the world remained anaemic and the high unemployment numbers dropped only very slowly. National debt levels rose in almost every country. Soon it became clear that the GFC and its ensuing Great Recession had spawned a severe *European Sovereign Debt Crisis* (ESDC) as well as a banking crisis. This rapidly escalating financial turmoil in the Eurozone not only threatened the fragile recovery of the global economy, but also came close to bankrupting the venerable birthplace of Western civilization—Greece.

Although the 2010s saw a slow process of recovery, the era of global instability continued. Some significant economic hiccups along the way included the 2016 Chinese stock market shock and the US–China trade war initiated by Donald Trump. In 2018, the

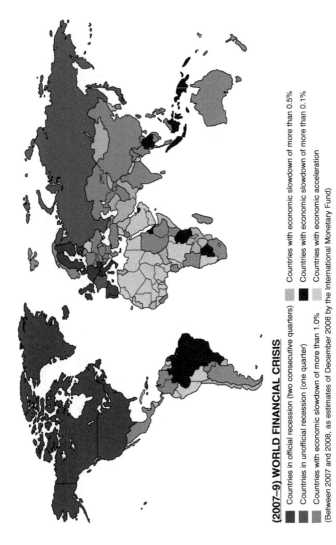

(2007–9) WORLD FINANCIAL CRISIS

- Countries in official recession (two consecutive quarters)
- Countries in unofficial recession (one quarter)
- Countries with economic slowdown of more than 1.0%
- Countries with economic slowdown of more than 0.5%
- Countries with economic slowdown of more than 0.1%
- Countries with economic acceleration

(Between 2007 and 2008, as estimates of December 2008 by the International Monetary Fund)

Map 3. Countries falling into recession as a result of the Global Financial Crisis, 2007–9.

The Greek debt crisis

The *Greek debt crisis* began in 2009 and 2010 when the Greek government announced that it had understated its national budget deficits for years and was running out of funds. Shut out from borrowing in global financial markets, the IMF and ECB were forced to put together two gigantic bailout packages totalling $275 billion in order to avoid the country's financial collapse. But the EU lenders imposed harsh austerity terms in exchange for the loan, which caused further economic hardship and failed to restore economic stability. Greece's economy shrank by a quarter and the national unemployment rate shot up to 25 per cent. For the entire decade of the 2010s, Greece had to rely on international creditors to keep its finances afloat, and tens of thousands of young people left the country in search of greater economic opportunities. While the Greek economy recorded a modest turnaround reflected in an annual growth rate of about 2 per cent from 2017 to 2020, most ordinary citizens complained that they were not feeling any significant improvement in their lives.

nationalist-populist US President imposed a series of trade tariffs on imported Chinese goods which led the Beijing regime headed by President Xi Jinping to answer with retaliatory tariffs. This dangerous escalation between the world's largest economies eased somewhat after the 2021 inauguration of President Joe Biden. By that time, however, a new, much more potent, economic threat had emerged from the shadows of illegal animal food markets in Wuhan, China: a global pandemic of the size and impact not seen since the so-called 'Spanish flu' in 1918.

The global spread of the SARS-2 coronavirus termed COVID-19 by the WHO (discussed in more detail in Chapter 8) caused severe economic shocks that included escalating unemployment numbers and plunging stock markets. In 2020, global trade and capital flows plummeted at the fastest pace on record. However, a year later, global trade in goods had rebounded and reached new record heights. In 2021, American consumers spent nearly $300 billion shopping via their cell phones. The DHL Connectedness Index—a major index measuring all four forms of globalization—shows that the pandemic hit embodied globalization the hardest as international tourist and business travel remained down more than 80 per cent in 2020–1. Still, since effective vaccines became available in 2021, most forecasts foresee international travel return to pre-pandemic levels by 2023, or, at the latest, 2024.

On the other hand, disembodied globalization surged ahead of all other forms as digital information flows spiked in response to in-person interactions going online to curb the spread of the coronavirus. While the DHL Report data show that the pandemic did not lead to the collapse of globalization, its enduring spillover effects included, for example, massive disruptions of global supply chains caused by extensive and repeated lockdowns in the manufacturing centres of China, congested sea ports around the world, disorganized shipping container management, and record freight rates.

Unsurprisingly, the world's poorest countries were impacted most severely by the health crisis. Falling far behind the speedy globalization recovery in wealthy regions, they experienced only an anaemic rebound of trade and foreign-direct investment flows. The dearth of support from the prosperous global North and limited access to COVID-19 vaccines proved to be additional factors hindering the post-pandemic recovery of the global South. In fact, the 50 least wealthy countries accounting for 21 per cent of the world's population only received 9 per cent of the vaccinations.

But thanks to swift action taken by governments and central banks, the global economy quickly rebounded to above pre-pandemic levels. G20 governments followed the advice of the IMF to maintain supportive monetary and fiscal policies to lessen the economic impact of the global recession. In particular, the IMF recommended a combination of accommodative monetary policies characterized by low interest rates and central bank programmes to facilitate credit availability, and fiscal support for individuals and firms. These measures included expanded unemployment insurance, tax cuts and tax deferrals for individuals and businesses, direct wage and income supplements to individuals; direct payments to businesses, and a massive infrastructure investment programme to promote growth. The US Congress approved historic fiscal spending packages totalling $5.1 trillion. The UK National Audit Office estimates that the UK government COVID package totalled £376 billion by 2022. Other governments around the world abandoned traditional borrowing caps in order to increase fiscal spending and return to economic growth. The IMF estimates that global fiscal support reached the unthinkable amount of $9 trillion by 2022.

However, these record investments in COVID-related aid did not come without a price. In late 2022, inflation surged to over 8 per cent in the EU, UK, US, and most other advanced market economies. In response, central banks raised their interest rates to increase the cost of borrowing money, thus reducing consumer demand. Four factors had pushed inflation to new heights. First, the huge fiscal support packages and swaths of government relief funds transferred to individuals and businesses enabled consumer spending to exceed its pre-pandemic levels. Second, as many workers were forced to work from home, spending shifted from in-person services to goods. The soaring consumer demand exceeded the production capacity of the goods sector. Third, global supply chain problems combined with surging production costs to raise the prices of most consumer items. Fourth, surging oil prices translated to dizzying rates at the pump—a development that was compounded by the massive oil and gas boycotts levelled against Russia in the wake of its 2022 Ukraine invasion. In addition, the Ukraine War sharply curtailed the ability of the two opponents to fulfil their role as the world's largest (Russia) and fourth-largest (Ukraine) grain exporters. Hence, food prices escalated especially in the global South, the largest consumers of Ukrainian and Russian agricultural products. But the full impact of the unprecedented global economic sanctions imposed on Russia has yet to materialize. What seems clear is that the era of global economic instability will continue for the foreseeable future.

The power of transnational corporations

Let us now return to our two remaining topics related to economic globalization: the growing power of TNCs and the enhanced role of international economic institutions. TNCs are the contemporary versions of the early modern commercial enterprises like the British East India Company, which we discussed in Chapter 2. They comprise the parent company and subsidiary units in more than one country, all of which operate under a coherent system of decision-making and a common strategy. TNC numbers skyrocketed from 7,000 in 1970 to over 100,000 in 2022. Enterprises like Apple, Meta, Google, Walmart, Sinopec Group, Amazon, Tesla, Saudi Aramco, Alibaba, and Toyota Motors belong to the world's 200 largest TNCs, and account for over half of the world's industrial output. Only few of these corporations maintain headquarters outside North America, Mexico, Saudi Arabia and the UAE, Europe, China, Japan, and South Korea. This geographical concentration reflects existing asymmetrical power relations between the global North and the South.

Rivalling nation-states in their economic power, these corporations control much of the world's investment capital, technology, and access to international markets. Headquartered in

57 countries and accounting for combined revenues of more than US$47 trillion, the top-2,000 TNCs on the *2022 Forbes Global 2000* list produced profits of $5 trillion, held assets worth $234 trillion, and represented a market value of $77 trillion. Measured by total market value, eight out of the top-10 TNCs are headquartered in the USA, including the No. 1 company, Apple. The top-10 TNCs could be placed easily in the top-25 bracket of the richest nations on Earth (see Table 1).

If we use *Forbes Global 2000* metrics based on a combination of sales, profits, assets, and market value, then only five companies are headquartered in the US while three are located in China, including the No. 2 company, the Industrial and Commercial Bank of China. Indeed, the gap between these two competing economic giants is shrinking: the US has 600 companies listed on the *2022 Forbes Global 2000* list of the world's 2,000 largest TNCs compared to China's 298.

Only a decade ago, the top-10 lists were dominated by oil companies such as ExxonMobil and physically located retailers such as Walmart. The speedy advance of digital technology has fundamentally changed the business landscape by creating room for a new type of firms based on enormous 'digital platforms'. Rather than confining themselves to being suppliers for goods, economic enterprises increasingly rely on these digital platforms to connect producers to consumers without themselves doing much producing or consuming. TNCs such as Meta, eBay, and Uber are good examples of the app-powered trend to attract and connect different customers to each other.

A matrix of intricate mathematical procedures known as 'algorithms' are playing a prominent role in globalized capitalism. Combined with AI, algorithms perform calculations, solve problems, and enable machine-learning. Algorithmic management is increasingly driving what has come to be known

Table 1. Transnational corporations versus countries: a comparison (2022)

Corporation	Industry/Headquarters	Total Market value (in US$ billion)	Country (global GDP rank)	GDP (in US$ billion)
1. Apple	Computer hardware, US	2,600	India (6)	2,670
2. Saudi Arabian Oil Company	Oil and gas operations, Saudi Arabia	2,400	France (7)	2,620
3. Microsoft	Computing software & programming, US	2,100	Italy (8)	1,890
4. Alphabet [Google]	Digital technology services, US	1,700	Canada (9)	1,650
5. Amazon.com	Retail & e-commerce, US	1,500	Russia (11)	1,480
6. Tesla	Electric vehicles, solar energy products, space commerce, US	864.7	Netherlands (18)	913
7. Berkshire Hathaway	Insurance, investment, US	735.2	Switzerland (19)	751
8. NVIDIA	Digital graphics processing, US	570	Poland (23)	597
9. Taiwan Semiconductor Manufacturing	Semiconductors, Taiwan	556	Sweden (24)	542
10. Meta Platforms [Facebook]	Social media platforms, US	545.4	Belgium (25)	522

as today's 'gig economy'. Its orientation towards short-term, temporary work without fringe benefits encourages giant firms to turn workers into 'independent contractors' who are seemingly masters of their own work-time. While promising 'flexibility', the AI-driven technology also accelerates the replacement of long-term jobs. For this reason, the 'automation' of the workplace has become a major topic in global economic discourse.

In order to maintain their command posts in the global marketplace, TNCs frequently merge with their competitors. In 2021, TNCs spent a whopping $5.9 trillion globally buying one another—the most since record-keeping began nearly four decades ago. Some of these mega-mergers include the 'mother of all beer mergers' uniting Anheuser-Busch InBev with SABMiller for the proud amount of US$105 billion in 2015; the US$130 billion marriage of Dow Chemical and DuPont in 2015; the US$278 billion consolidation of China's biggest coal miner, Shenhua Group, with China Guodian Corporation, the country's largest coal-fired power generators, in 2017; and the US$121 billion union of United Technologies (Aerospace Division) with giant arms manufacturer and major US defence contractor Raytheon in 2019.

TNCs have consolidated their global operations in what has remained a largely deregulated global labour market. The availability of cheap labour, resources, and favourable production conditions in the global South has enhanced corporate mobility and profitability. Accounting for over 70 per cent of world trade, TNCs are responsible for massive foreign direct investments (FDI). As the 2022 UNCTAD *World Investment Report* shows, global FDI undertaken by transnational enterprises in 2021 reached $1.6 trillion.

No doubt, the immense power of TNCs has profoundly altered the structure and functioning of the world economy. These giant firms and their global strategies have become major determinants of trade flows, the location of industries, and other economic activities around the world. In particular, their ability to disperse manufacturing processes into many discrete phases carried out in many different locations around the world has globalized economic production. Immense transnational production networks allow TNCs like Walmart, General Motors, or Volkswagen to break down the production process into detachable component phases that can be dispersed throughout the world. Such global value chains also allow for a faster and more efficient distribution and marketing of their products on a global scale (see Map 4). As previously discussed, these chains have come under immense strain as a result of the COVID-19 pandemic.

A groundbreaking study published in 2011 analysed the relationships between 43,060 large TNCs in terms of share ownerships linking them. The findings revealed that a relatively small core of 1,318 corporations appeared to own collectively through their shares the majority of the world's large blue chip and manufacturing firms. In fact, an even smaller number of these TNCS—147 super-connected corporations, to be exact—controlled 40 per cent of the total wealth in the network. Most of them were financial institutions like Barclays Bank, which topped the list. Ironically, it was this very bank that found itself at the centre of a huge scandal that rocked the financial world in July 2012, when it was revealed that Barclays and 15 other major banks had rigged the world's most important global interest rate for years. Similarly, Walmart admitted in 2019 to violating the US Foreign Corrupt Practices Act by making illegal bribery payments to foreign government officials in order to open new production locations around the globe at extremely favourable terms. Walmart's guilty plea resulted in a US$282 million fine, a rather paltry figure compared to its massive US$7 billion profit generated in 2018.

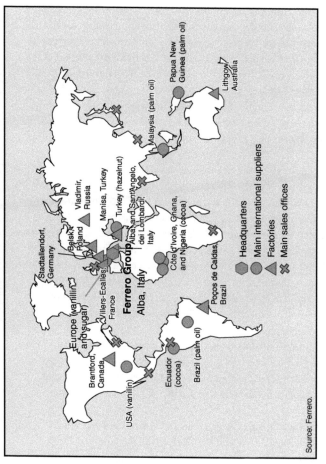

Source: Ferrero.

Map 4. The Nutella® global value chain.

The enhanced role of international economic institutions

Formed in 1999, the Group of 20 (G20) constitutes perhaps the most influential global economic forum in the world today. It comprises the 20 most powerful national economies representing more than 80 per cent of world GDP but only 60 per cent of the world's population. Its annual summits allow government leaders to meet regularly and discuss major economic and political issues. As we noted, emergency G20 meetings can be called to discuss and coordinate collective economic responses to global crises like the GFC or the COVID-19 pandemic.

In addition, three international economic institutions most frequently mentioned in the context of economic globalization are the IMF, the World Bank, and the WTO. These institutions enjoy the privileged position of making and enforcing the rules of a global economy that is sustained by significant power differentials between the global North and South. Since we will discuss the WTO in some detail in Chapter 7, let us focus here on the other two institutions. As pointed out, the IMF and the World Bank emerged from the BWR. During the Cold War, their important function of providing loans for developing countries became connected to the West's political objective of containing communism. Starting in the 1970s, and especially after the fall of the Soviet Union, the economic agenda of the IMF and the World Bank largely supported neoliberal interests to integrate and deregulate markets around the world.

In return for supplying much-needed loans to developing countries, the IMF and the World Bank demand from their creditor nations the implementation of so-called *structural adjustment programmes* (SAPs). Unleashed on developing countries in the 1990s, this set of neoliberal policies is often referred to as the 'Washington Consensus' (WC). It was devised and codified by John Williamson, who was an IMF adviser in the 1970s. The various sections of the WC were mainly directed at countries with large foreign debts remaining from the 1970s and 1980s. The official purpose of Williamson's framework was to reform the internal economic mechanisms of debtor countries in the developing world so that they would be in a better position to repay the debts they had incurred. In practice, however, the terms of the WC spelled out a new form of colonialism. Its 10 points, as defined by Williamson, required governments to implement the following SAPs in order to qualify for loans:

1. A guarantee of fiscal discipline, and a curb to budget deficits.
2. A reduction of public expenditure, particularly in the military and public administration.
3. Tax reform, aiming at the creation of a system with a broad base and with effective enforcement.
4. Financial liberalization, with interest rates determined by the market.
5. Competitive exchange rates, to assist export-led growth.
6. Trade liberalization, coupled with the abolition of import licensing and a reduction of tariffs.
7. Promotion of foreign direct investment.
8. Privatization of state enterprises, leading to efficient management and improved performance.
9. Deregulation of the economy.
10. Protection of property rights.

It is no coincidence that this programme is called the WC, for, from the outset, the United States has been the dominant power in the IMF and the World Bank.

Unfortunately, however, large portions of the 'development loans' granted by these institutions have either been pocketed by authoritarian political leaders in the global South or have enriched local businesses and the Northern corporations they usually serve. Sometimes, exorbitant sums are spent on ill-considered construction projects. Most importantly, however, SAPs rarely produce the desired result of developing debtor societies, because mandated cuts in public spending translate into fewer social programmes, reduced educational opportunities, more environmental pollution, and greater poverty for the vast majority of people.

Typically, the largest share of the developing countries' national budget is spent on servicing their outstanding debts. A 2018 analysis from Jubilee Debt Campaign shows that average government external debt payments across the 126 developing countries for which data were available increased to 10.7 per cent of government revenue in 2017, the highest level since 2004. According to comprehensive World Bank and OECD data, developing countries paid out, in 2019, $744 billion in debt service while receiving only $164 billion in aid. The total external debt of emerging and developing countries skyrocketed from US$70.2 billion in 1970 to US$8.7 trillion in 2020. This sounds like a lot of money, but it represents less than 30 per cent of the estimated $29 trillion the US government spent on the bailout of the banks in the wake of the 2008 GFC. Pressured for decades by anti-corporate globalist forces like the Committee for the Abolition of Third-World Debt or the Jubilee Debt Campaign, the IMF and the World Bank have only recently been willing to consider a new policy of blanket debt forgiveness in special cases.

To sum up, this chapter has made a strong case for the significance of economics and technology in our exploration of globalization. But we ought to be sceptical of one-sided accounts that identify expanding economic activity as the primary aspect of globalization. Moreover, economic and technological dimensions of globalization are also closely connected to political processes. As the activities of global institutions such as G20 illustrate, the forging of global economic connections involves a series of related political decisions. For this reason, we now turn to a discussion of the political dimension of globalization.

Chapter 4
The political dimension of globalization

Political globalization refers to the intensification and expansion of political interrelations across the globe. These processes raise an important set of political issues pertaining to the principle of state sovereignty, the growing impact of intergovernmental organizations, the future prospects for regional and global governance, demographics, and global migration flows. Obviously, these themes respond to the evolution of political arrangements beyond the framework of the nation-state, thus breaking new conceptual and institutional ground.

For the last two centuries, humans have organized their political differences along territorial lines that generated a sense of 'belonging' to a particular nation-state. Based on 17th-century European principles of sovereignty and territoriality, the modern nation-state system found its mature expression at the end of the First World War in US President Woodrow Wilson's famous *Fourteen Points* of national self-determination. But Wilson's assumption that all forms of national identity should be given their territorial expression in a sovereign nation-state proved to be extremely difficult to enforce in practice. Moreover, by enshrining the nation-state as the ethical and legal pinnacle of his proposed interstate system, he unwittingly lent some legitimacy to those radical ethnonationalist forces that pushed the world into the Second World War.

This artificial division of planetary social space into 'domestic' and 'foreign' spheres corresponds to people's national imaginary that engenders collective identities based on the creation of a hostile binary: 'us' versus 'them'. Thus, the modern nation-state system has rested on psychological foundations and cultural assumptions that convey a sense of existential security and historic continuity of the national, while at the same time demanding from its citizens that they put their patriotic loyalties to the ultimate test. Nurtured by demonizing images of 'outsiders' and 'foreigners', people's belief in the superiority of their own nation has supplied the psychological energy required for large-scale warfare—just as the enormous productive capacities of the modern state have provided the material means necessary to fight the costly *total wars* of the last century.

President Wilson's other main idea of a *League of Nations* that would give international cooperation an institutional expression was belatedly realized with the founding of the *United Nations* in 1945 (see Figure 9). While deeply rooted in a political order based

9. The Security Council of the United Nations in session.

on the modern nation-state system, the UN and other fledgling intergovernmental organizations also served as catalysts for the gradual extension of political activities across national boundaries, thus simultaneously affirming and undermining the principle of national sovereignty.

As globalization grew stronger during the 1980s and 1990s, the international order of separate nation-states encountered a worldwide web of political interdependencies that challenged conventional forms of national sovereignty. Noticing these tendencies, many globalization experts have suggested that the period since the 1990s has been marked by a radical deterritorialization of politics, rule-making, and governance. Since then, three fundamental questions probe the extent of political globalization. First, is it really true that the power of the nation-state has been curtailed by massive flows of capital, people, and technology across territorial boundaries? Second, are the primary causes of these flows to be found in politics or in economics? Third, are we witnessing the emergence of new global governance structures? This chapter will consider them in turn.

The demise of the nation-state?

Two opposing perspectives—*hyperglobalist* and *sceptical*—offer different assessments of the fate of the modern nation-state based on diverging views on the relative importance of political factors. *Hyperglobalizers* seek to convince the public that globalization inevitably involves the decline of bounded territory as a meaningful concept for understanding political and social change. They consider political globalization a secondary phenomenon driven by more fundamental economic and technological forces. For example, since the workings of global capital markets curtail the ability of governments to control exchange rates or protect their currency, nation-states have become vulnerable to the discipline imposed by economic choices made on a supranational level. Promoting the image of globalization as an irreversible juggernaut flattening the nation-state, hyperglobalizers argue that nation-states have already lost their dominant role in the global economy. Celebrating the alleged rise of a 'borderless world', they look forward to a new phase in world history in which the main role of government will be to serve as a superconductor for global capitalism.

Considering such pronouncements premature at best and erroneous at worst, *globalization sceptics* have not only affirmed the continued dominance of the nation-state as the political container of modern social life but also pointed to the emergence of regional blocs as evidence for new forms of subglobal territorialization. They highlight the central role of politics in unleashing the forces of globalization, especially through the successful mobilization of political power. Once pro-market political decisions were implemented, worldwide economic integration and supportive new technologies came into their own. The clear implication of this sceptical perspective is that national territory still matters.

The arguments of both hyperglobalizers and sceptics remain entangled in a particularly vexing version of the chicken-and-the-egg problem. After all, economic forms of interdependence are set in motion by political decisions, but these decisions are nonetheless made in particular economic contexts. For example, it has become much easier for capital to escape taxation schemes and other national policy restrictions. In 2016, the *Panama Papers*—a leaked set of nearly 12 million confidential documents—revealed how wealthy individuals, including government officials, managed to evade national income taxes by hiding their assets in Panamanian offshore companies. Moreover, global markets frequently undermine the capacity of governments to set independent national policy objectives and impose their own domestic standards. While it seems obvious to acknowledge the decline of the nation-state as a sovereign entity and the ensuing devolution of state power to both local governments and supranational institutions, the current surge of national populism described in Chapter 7 suggests that political globalization is not an irreversible process.

Demographics, urbanization, and migration

The relative decline of the nation-state over the last three decades does not necessarily mean that national governments have become impotent bystanders to the workings of global forces. States still constitute the primary political framework in the world today and they have continued to retain control over education, infrastructure, and foreign policy. One of the major challenges facing states is demographic. Some countries will have to accommodate more citizens whereas others will have to cope with a net population loss and an ageing citizenry. The world's population will continue to increase every year, adding about 1.4 billion people to reach an estimated total population of 9.2 billion by 2040. Most of the increase will occur in the global South, with Sub-Saharan Africa absorbing nearly two-thirds of the growth. Since developing countries already struggle to meet the basic needs of their population, the exploding number of young people with few educational and work prospects will add to the political volatility and security problems of these regions.

Second, the world's urban population is expected to rise from 56 per cent in 2020 to 66 per cent in 2040, with nearly all of the growth accruing in the developing world. The UN projects that 8 out of the 10 largest cities will be located in the global South. The top six urban centres in 2040—Mumbai, India; Delhi, India; Dhaka, Bangladesh; Kinshasa, Democratic Republic of Congo; Kolkata, India; and Lagos, Nigeria—will have to accommodate over 32 million inhabitants each. The associated sprawl of urban slums is bound to have not only devastating social and environmental impacts, but will also put tremendous strain on the governance relations between city councils and national political institutions.

Finally, intensifying population movements within and across countries present another challenge to some of the most crucial powers of nation-states: immigration control, population registration, and security protocols. From 2001 to 2020, the proportion of the world's population living outside their birth country increased from 2.8 per cent to 3.6 per cent, its highest level on record. The number of international migrants reached 281 million in 2020, which represents an increase of over 100 million since 2000 (see Figure C). In addition to millions of people fleeing disasters and conflict, demographic trends and economic incentives will continue to drive large-scale migration for decades to come. With about 3.6 per cent of the world's population living outside their country of origin in 2021, immigration control has become a central issue in most advanced nations. Many governments seek to restrict population flows, particularly those originating in the poor countries of the global South. In the United States, annual inflows of about 1.2 million legal permanent immigrants during the 2010s are surpassed by the estimated 1.6 million undocumented migrants entering the country. The US-based Center for Immigration Studies reports that the total number of illegal immigrants in the country in 2022 surpassed the 11 million mark.

The growing problems of nation-states to cope with increasing transborder migration flows have been on constant display for many years. Let us consider the following challenging example: the *Syrian refugee crisis*. It started in the early 2010s when the Syrian dictator Bashar al-Assad, backed by authoritarian Russian President Vladimir Putin, embarked on a confrontational course with domestic pro-democracy 'Arab Spring' demonstrators whom he vilified as 'rebel forces'. The country quickly descended into an all-out civil war that would kill more than 250,000 people over the next five years. The relentless fighting triggered a humanitarian crisis of truly epic proportions. By 2016, nearly 6 million Syrians—out of a total population of 23 million—had been internally displaced; 5 million people had fled the country in search

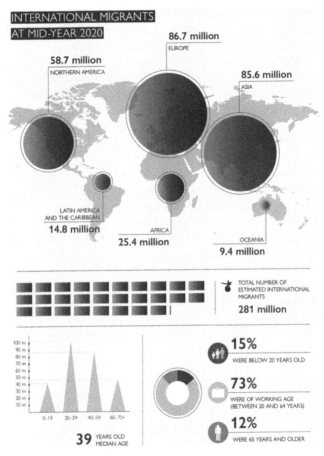

C. Number of international migrants, 2020.

of both personal safety and economic opportunity (see Map 5). The majority of Syrian refugees ended up in camps in the neighbouring countries of Jordan, Lebanon, Iraq, and Turkey. But more than a million people attempted the dangerous trip across the Mediterranean from Turkey to Greece, hoping to find a better future in the prosperous states of the European Union, especially Germany.

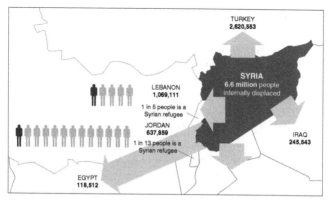

Map 5. The Syrian refugee crisis.

The Syrian refugee crisis also revealed the inadequacy of the EU's current institutional immigration arrangements based on national preferences. The *Schengen Agreement* which provides for open borders among EU core countries lacks the robustness and comprehensiveness necessary for coping with a migration crisis of this magnitude. As policy differences among various national governments became more pronounced, some member countries temporarily withdrew from the agreement and reinstituted stricter border controls. Others placed arbitrary limits on the number of refugees they were willing to process and refused to consider a more coordinated approach.

Moreover, the Syrian refugee crisis also made visible existing cultural fissures and religious biases. For example, a number of official government ministers in EU member states like Poland, Slovakia, and Hungary openly expressed their opposition to the 'Islamization of Europe' and signalled their acceptance of only a small number of Christian refugees. However, when more than 5 million Ukrainian refugees were forced to leave their country in the wake of the 2022 Russian invasion of their homeland, Poland generously welcomed 3.5 million of their displaced Christian neighbours. There is much evidence that cultural and religious bias impacts political decisions. For example, the pro-Brexit forces in the UK used the Syrian refugee crisis in their 2016 referendum campaign to convince the British people that the only way to stop Muslim mass immigration was to leave the EU.

But the Syrian refugee crisis represents only the most massive case among similar migration movements around the world. According to 2021 UN figures, a record 84 million refugees have been forced to flee their homes—despite the conditions of reduced mobility as a result of the COVID-19 pandemic. Examples include the forced expulsion of an estimated 1.1 million Rohingya people—an Islamic minority in Myanmar excluded from citizenship—as well as hundreds of thousands of Central American refugees who have sought political asylum in the USA. The latter case, in particular, drew much attention during the 2017–21 presidency of Donald Trump. Many people around the world were shocked that one of the world's most liberal immigration countries would apply a so-called *zero-tolerance approach* designed to deter illegal migration by legitimate political refugees seeking to escape the deadly violence in their home countries. In fact, the Trump administration went so far as to forcibly separate thousands of children from their families. Kept under egregious conditions in migrant detention facilities that have been compared to 'concentration camps' by some critics, many of these children were ultimately transferred into foster care placement across the US—without their parents' permission and no adequate tracking mechanisms that would allow for a safe reunion with their families (see Figure 10). While the new Biden administration repealed the zero-tolerance measure and managed to improve the dire situation in the camps, the early 2020s saw new waves of Central American refugees arrive at the US–Mexican border.

Finally, the intensifying global migration dynamics also play into crucial issues of *national security*. For example, the heinous attacks of global terrorist networks affiliated with jihadist Islamist groups like ISIL or al-Shabaab—such as the 2017 Manchester

10. Central American migrants, including children, behind the fence of a makeshift US detention centre in El Paso, Texas, 29 March 2019.

Arena bombing, the 2018 suicide bombings in the Nigerian city of Mubi, or the deadly 2019 Sri Lanka Easter bombings—have revealed the inadequacy of conventional national security routines and protocols. As a result, the globalization of terrorist and crime networks has forced nation-states to engage in new forms of international cooperation. Thus, we can observe the seemingly paradoxical effect of political globalization: while states still matter, they are pushed to hammer out new global agreements that might undermine their old claims to sovereignty and non-interference.

In summary, then, we ought to reject premature pronouncements of the impending demise of the nation-state, while also acknowledging its increasing difficulties in performing many of its traditional functions. Contemporary globalization has weakened some of the conventional boundaries between domestic and foreign policies while fostering the growth of supraterritorial social spaces and institutions that, in turn, unsettle both familiar political arrangements and cultural traditions. As the 21st century

Losing national control? Russia's interference in the 2016 US Presidential election

The Russian government's systematic and sweeping attempts to influence the 2016 US presidential election in favour of Donald Trump represents another instructive case of how nation-states are struggling to maintain control over even their most basic functions such as the organization and management of open and fair national elections. The official 2019 report issued by Special Counsel Robert S. Mueller III established that Russia interfered in the election principally through two operations. First, a Russian entity carried out a social media campaign that favoured presidential candidate Donald J. Trump and disparaged presidential candidate Hillary Clinton. Second, a Russian intelligence service conducted computer-intrusion operations against entities, employees, and volunteers working on the Clinton Campaign and then released stolen documents.

wears on, people around the world will become more conscious of the fact that they live in a transitional era in which the modern nation-state system will be increasingly challenged by global problems that require strengthening the dynamics of global governance structures.

Political globalization and global governance

Political globalization is perhaps most visible in the rise of supraterritorial institutions and associations like the International Criminal Court or the International Law Commission held together by common norms and interests (see Figure D). In this early phase of *global governance*, these structures resemble an eclectic network of interrelated power centres such as municipal and provincial authorities, regional blocs, international organizations, and national and international private-sector associations.

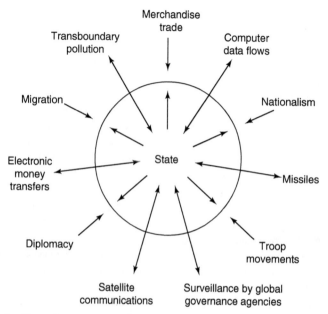

Merchandise trade

Transboundary pollution

Computer data flows

Migration

Nationalism

Electronic money transfers

State

Missiles

Diplomacy

Troop movements

Satellite communications

Surveillance by global governance agencies

D. The nation-state in a globalizing world.

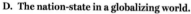

On the municipal and provincial level, there has been a remarkable growth in the number of policy initiatives and transborder links between various substate authorities. For example, Chinese provinces and US federal states have established permanent missions and points of contact, some of which operate relatively autonomously with little oversight from their respective national governments. Various provinces and federal states in Canada, India, and Brazil are developing their own trade agendas and financial strategies to obtain loans. An example of international cooperation on the municipal level is the rise of powerful city networks such as the World Association of Major Metropolises that develop cooperative ventures to deal with common local issues across national borders. So-called *global cities*—Hong Kong, London, New York, Shanghai, Singapore, Johannesburg, Tokyo, and many others—are in some respects more closely connected to each other than they are to their national governments.

On the regional level, there has been an extraordinary proliferation of multilateral organizations and agreements. Regional clubs and transnational agencies such as APEC or ASEAN have sprung up across the world, leading some observers to speculate that regional networks will eventually replace nation-states as the basic unit of governance. Starting out as attempts to integrate regional economies, these blocs have, in some cases, already evolved into loose political federations with common institutions of governance. For example, the European common market began in 1950 with French Foreign Minister Robert Schuman's modest plan to create a supranational institution charged with regulating French and German coal and steel production. Seven decades on, the 28 member states of the EU form a close community with some shared political institutions that create common public policies and design binding security arrangements. In the first decade of the 21st century, several formerly communist countries joined the EU, which now extends as far to the east as Latvia, Romania, and Cyprus (see Map 6). And it might be even further enlarged. In the wake of the 2022 Russian invasion, Ukraine and the Republic of Moldova were granted membership candidate status by EU leaders. But, as we discuss further in Chapter 8, such an expansionist dynamic is by no means inexorable. Brexit is a clear illustration that even a decade-long process of regionalization can be halted and possibly reversed.

On a global level, governments have formed a number of international organizations, including the UN, NATO, WTO, and OECD. Full legal membership in these organizations is open to states only, and the decision-making authority lies with representatives from national governments. The proliferation of

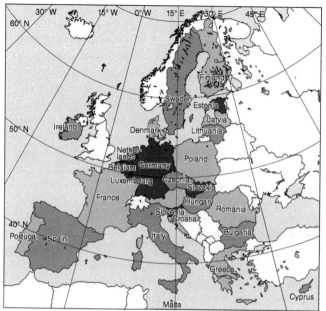

Map 6. The European Union, 2020.

these transnational bodies has shown that nation-states find it increasingly difficult to manage sprawling networks of social interdependence.

Toward a global civil society?

Finally, the emerging structure of global governance has been shaped by *global civil society*—a shared social realm populated by thousands of voluntary, non-governmental associations of worldwide reach. International NGOs such as Doctors Without Borders or Greenpeace represent millions of ordinary citizens who are prepared to challenge political and economic decisions made by nation-states and intergovernmental organizations.

One concrete example of the growing significance of INGOs in managing increasing global interconnectivity was the role of *Médecins Sans Frontières*/Doctors Without Borders (MSF/DWB) during the dramatic outbreak of the Ebola virus disease in West Africa in the 2010s. Made up mainly of doctors and health sector workers from around the world who volunteer their services at any location on earth, MSF/DWB provides assistance to populations in distress such as victims of natural and man-made disasters, and armed conflict. It observes neutrality and impartiality in the name of its universal medical code of ethics and also maintains complete independence from all political, economic, and religious powers.

As a result of the tough lessons learned in the struggle against global pandemics like Ebola and COVID-19, some Global Studies experts believe that political globalization might facilitate the strengthening of democratic transnational social forces anchored in this thriving sphere of global civil society. Predicting that democratic rights will ultimately become detached from their narrow relationship to discrete territorial units such as nation-states, these optimistic voices anticipate the creation of a democratic global governance structure based on Western cosmopolitan ideals, international legal arrangements, and a web of expanding linkages between various governmental and non-governmental organizations. If such a promising prospect indeed comes to pass, then the final outcome of political globalization might well be the emergence of a *cosmopolitan democracy* that would constitute the basis for a plurality of identities flourishing within a structure of mutual toleration and accountability (see Figure E).

According to the late David Held, one of the chief academic proponents of this view, such a cosmopolitan democracy of the future would contain the following features:

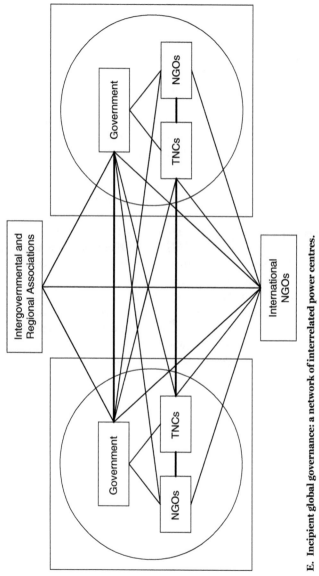

E. Incipient global governance: a network of interrelated power centres.

1. A global parliament connected to regions, states, and localities;
2. A new charter of rights and duties locked into different domains of political, social, and economic power;
3. The formal separation of political and economic interests;
4. An interconnected global legal system with mechanisms of enforcement from the local to the global.

A number of less optimistic commentators have challenged Held's idea that political globalization is moving in the direction of cosmopolitan democracy, especially in light of the populist backlash against globalization and the rise of authoritarianism in the world. Most criticisms of Held's hopeful vision of more cosmopolitan political arrangements boil down to the charge that it represents a utopian idealism that does not take seriously enough the enduring political tensions on the national level of public policy such as the clashing immigration perspectives we discussed above. Global governance sceptics have also expressed the suspicion that the proponents of cosmopolitan democracy have not considered in sufficient detail its cultural feasibility. In other words, the worldwide intensification of cultural interactions makes the possibility of political resistance and opposition just as real as the benign vision of mutual accommodation and tolerance of differences. To follow up on this cultural dimension of globalization, let us turn to Chapter 5.

Chapter 5
The cultural dimension of globalization

Cultural globalization refers to the intensification and expansion of cultural flows across the globe. Obviously, *culture* is a very broad concept. Referring to patterns of meaning and ways of life, it is frequently used to describe the whole of human experience. In order to avoid the ensuing danger of overgeneralization, it is important to make analytical distinctions between various aspects of social life. For example, we associate the adjective 'economic' with the production, exchange, and consumption of commodities. If we are discussing the 'political', we mean practices related to the generation and distribution of power in societies. If we are talking about the 'cultural', we are concerned with the symbolic construction, articulation, and dissemination of meaning. Given that language, music, and images constitute the major forms of symbolic expression, they assume special significance for the dynamics of cultural interactions.

The exploding network of cultural interconnections in the last decades has led some commentators to suggest that such practices lie at the very heart of contemporary globalization. Yet, cultural globalization did not start with the worldwide dissemination of rock'n'roll, Coca-Cola, or football. As noted in Chapter 2, expansive civilizational exchanges are much older than modernity. Still, both the volume and extent of cultural transmissions in the 21st century have far exceeded those of earlier times.

Turbocharged by expanding social media platforms and our proliferating mobile digital devices, the dominant symbolic systems of meaning of our global age—such as individualism, consumerism, and various religious discourses—circulate more freely and widely than ever before. As images, ideas, and information can be more easily and rapidly transmitted from one place to another, they profoundly impact the way people experience their everyday lives. As we saw in our lost cell phone story in Chapter 3, cultural practices have escaped the prison of fixed localities such as town and nation, eventually acquiring new *glocal* meanings in interaction with dominant global themes.

The thematic landscape traversed by scholars of cultural globalization is vast and the questions they raise are too numerous to be fleshed out in this very short introduction. Rather than offering a long laundry list of relevant topics, this chapter will focus on three important themes: the tension between sameness and difference in the emerging global culture; the crucial role of transnational media corporations in disseminating popular culture; and the globalization of languages.

Global culture: sameness or difference?

Does globalization make people around the world more alike or more different? This is the question most frequently raised in discussions on the subject of cultural globalization. A group of commentators we might call *pessimistic globalizers* argue in favour of the former. They suggest that we are not moving towards a cultural rainbow that reflects the diversity of the world's existing populations. Rather, we are witnessing the rise of an increasingly homogenized popular culture underwritten by a Western 'culture industry' based in New York, Hollywood, London, Paris, and Milan. As evidence for their interpretation, these commentators point to Amazonian Indians wearing Nike sneakers; denizens of the southern Sahara purchasing Yankees baseball caps; and Palestinian youths proudly displaying their Golden State Warriors basketball singlets in downtown Ramallah. This portrayal of globalization as a ruthless homogenizing force spreading the logic of Anglo-American capitalism and Western values at the expense of local and national cultures has become very influential. It has appeared as the spectre of *Americanization* stalking vulnerable regions of the world. Although there have been serious attempts by some countries to resist what is often referred to as 'cultural imperialism'—for example, a ban on satellite dishes in Iran, China's Internet censorship system, and the French imposition of tariffs and quotas on imported films and television programmes—the spread of American popular culture seems to be unstoppable.

But these manifestations of sameness are also evident inside the dominant countries of the global North. American sociologist George Ritzer coined the term *McDonaldization* to describe the wide-ranging sociocultural processes by which the principles of the fast-food restaurant are coming to dominate more and more sectors of American society as well as the rest of the world. On the surface, these principles appear to be rational in their attempts to offer efficient and predictable ways of serving people's needs.

However, looking behind the façade of repetitive TV commercials that claim to 'love to see you smile', we can identify a number of serious problems. For one, the generally low nutritional value of fast-food meals—and particularly their high fat content—has been implicated in the rise of serious health problems such as heart disease, diabetes, cancer, and juvenile obesity (see Table 2). Moreover, the idea that impersonal, routine operations of 'rational' fast-service establishments actually apply to the rest of the world undermines expressions of *cultural diversity*. In the long run, the McDonaldization of the world amounts to the imposition of uniform standards that eclipse human creativity and dehumanize social relations. In order to expand markets and make more profit, global capitalists are developing homogeneous global products targeting especially the young and wealthy throughout the world, as well as turning children into avid consumers from a very early

Table 2. The American way of life, 2017–22

Average daily time Americans spend watching TV (in minutes in 2021)	197
Average daily time Americans spend communicating face to face (in minutes in 2021)	52
Average daily time Americans spend on mobile devices (in minutes in 2022)	174
Number of advertisements, logos, and labels seen by the average American every day (2017)	4,000–10,000
Percentage of adult Americans who are obese (2020)	41.9%
Average annual intake of meat per person in the US vs India (in kg in 2018)	101 vs 4
Average annual meat intake per person in US equals how many hamburgers (2018)	800
Average number of different cows in a single fast-food hamburger	100+
Food wasted in America in 2022 (in million tonnes)	40
Number of Americans who are food insecure in 2022 (in millions)	50
Number of cars registered in the US (in millions in 2021)	289.5
Amount of rubbish produced by Americans (in million tonnes in 2018)	292.4
Total mass of living humans on Earth (in million tonnes in 2017)	287
Percentage of Americans who believe that God created humans in their present form less than 10,000 years ago (2019)	40%

Total US population (in millions in 2018) vs number of civilian-held firearms in the US (in millions in 2018)	329 vs 393
Percentage of civilian-held firearms in the US as share of the worldwide total of firearms (2018)	46%
Annual number of people killed by firearms in the US vs UK (2019)	37,038 vs 155

11. Jihad versus McWorld: selling fast food in Indonesia.

age. Thus, global consumerism becomes an increasingly soulless and unethical cultural framework.

While *optimistic globalizers* agree with their pessimistic colleagues that cultural globalization generates more sameness, they nonetheless consider this pattern of sameness to be a good thing. American social theorist Francis Fukuyama explicitly welcomes the global spread of Anglo-American values and lifestyles, equating the Americanization of the world with the desirable expansion of democracy and free markets (see Figure 11). But optimistic globalizers do not just come in the form of American nationalists who apply the old national theme of *manifest destiny* to the global arena. Still, some representatives of this camp consider themselves staunch cosmopolitans who celebrate social media and the latest digital devices as harbingers of a homogenized techno-culture. Others are unabashed free-market enthusiasts who embrace the values of global consumer capitalism.

While acknowledging globalization's homogenization dynamic, we should also note its tendencies towards cultural diversification and hybridization. It is one thing to acknowledge the existence of powerful sameness tendencies in the world, but it is quite another to assert that most cultural diversity existing on our planet is destined to vanish. In fact, several influential commentators offer a contrary assessment that links globalization to multiplying forms of cultural expression. The late sociologist Roland Robertson, for example, contends that global cultural flows often reinvigorate local cultural niches. The result is often visible in the proliferation of culturally specific festivals and large urban parades celebrating marginalized values represented by such groups as the LGBTQ+ community.

Hence, rather than being totally obliterated by the Western consumerist forces of sameness, local difference and particularity still play an important role in creating unique cultural constellations. Arguing that cultural globalization always takes place in local contexts, Global Studies scholars like Jan Nederveen Pieterse reject the cultural homogenization thesis and speak instead of *glocalization*—a complex dynamic involving the interaction of the global and local we discussed in previous chapters. The resulting expressions of *hybridity* cannot be reduced to clear-cut manifestations of 'sameness' or 'difference'. Such processes of *cultural hybridization* have become most visible in fashion, music, dance, film, food, sports, and language.

But the respective arguments of optimistic and pessimistic globalizers are not necessarily incompatible. The contemporary experience of living and acting across cultural borders often means both the loss of traditional meanings and the creation of new symbolic expressions. Reconstructed feelings of belonging coexist in uneasy tension with a sense of placelessness. Other commentators like the late sociologist Ulrich Beck have pointed to the rapid increase of *place-bigamists*—people whose enhanced mobility allows them to feel at home in more than just one place. Seen from this perspective, it appears that a homogenized form of modernity is actually giving way to a new *postmodern* framework characterized by a less stable sense of identity, place, meaning, and knowledge.

Given the complexity of global cultural flows, one would actually expect to see uneven and contradictory effects. In certain contexts, these flows might change traditional manifestations of national identity in the direction of a popular culture characterized by sameness; in others they might foster new expressions of cultural particularism; in still others they might encourage forms of cultural hybridity. Those commentators who summarily denounce the homogenizing effects of Americanization must not forget that hardly any society in our globalizing world possesses an 'authentic', self-contained culture. In fact, cultural hybridity seems to be ubiquitous in today's globalizing world. Think, for example, of the emotional exuberance of Bollywood movies, the intricacy of several variations of Hawaiian pidgin, the culinary delights of Cuban-Chinese cuisine. Finally, those who applaud the spread of consumerist capitalism also need to pay attention to its negative consequences, such as the dramatic decline of traditional communal folkways as well as the commodification of society and nature.

The role of the media

To a large extent, the global cultural flows of our time are generated and directed by sprawling media empires that rely on powerful communication technologies to spread their message. As we discussed in Chapter 3, *media* covers a wide variety of streams—advertising, broadcasting and networking, news, print and publication, digital, recording, and motion pictures. Saturating global cultural reality with formulaic TV shows and mindless advertisements, these corporations increasingly shape people's identities and the structure of desires around the world. The rise of the global imaginary is inextricably connected to the rise of the global media. During the last two decades, a small group of gigantic TNCs have come to dominate the global market for entertainment, news, television, and film. In 2022, the world's eight largest media conglomerates—Comcast, Disney, Charter Communications, Netflix, Paramount, Naspers Limited Class N, DISH Network Class A, and Liberty Global Class A—accounted for more than two-thirds of the $2.5 trillion in annual worldwide revenues generated by the global telecommunications industry.

As recently as the turn of the millennium, many of today's giant dominant corporations did not exist in their present form as all-encompassing media companies. Today, most media analysts concede that the emergence of a global commercial-media market amounts to the creation of a global oligopoly similar to that of the oil and automotive industries in the early part of the 20th century. The crucial cultural innovators of earlier decades—small, independent record labels, radio stations, movie theatres, newspapers, and book publishers—have become virtually extinct as they have found themselves incapable of competing with today's media giants.

The commercial values disseminated by transnational media enterprises not only secure the undisputed cultural hegemony of popular culture, but also can lead to the depoliticization of social reality and the weakening of civic bonds. One of the most glaring developments of the last two decades has been the transformation of news broadcasts and educational programmes into shallow entertainment shows—many of them ironically touted as 'reality shows' such as *The Apprentice*, which ran in the US on NBC across 14 seasons and served as the publicity foundation for Donald Trump's successful 2016 presidential campaign.

Given that news is less than half as profitable as entertainment, media firms are increasingly tempted to pursue higher profits by ignoring journalism's much vaunted separation of newsroom practices and business decisions. Partnerships and alliances between news and entertainment companies are fast becoming the norm, making it more common for publishing executives to press journalists to cooperate with their newspapers' business operations. Sustained attacks on the professional autonomy of journalists, which accuse them of spreading 'fake news', are, therefore, also part of cultural globalization.

The globalization of languages

One direct method of measuring and evaluating cultural changes brought about by globalization is to study the shifting global patterns of language use. The globalization of languages can be viewed as a process by which some languages are increasingly used in international communication while others lose their prominence and even disappear for lack of speakers. Researchers at the Globalization Research Center at the University of Hawai'i have identified five key variables that influence the globalization of languages:

1. *Number of languages:* The declining number of languages in different parts of the world points to the strengthening of homogenizing cultural forces.

2. *Movements of people:* People carry their languages with them when they migrate and travel. Migration patterns affect the spread of languages.

3. *Foreign language learning and tourism:* Foreign language learning and tourism facilitate the spread of languages beyond national or cultural boundaries.

4. *Internet languages:* The Internet has become a global medium for instant communication and quick access to information. Language use on the Internet is a key factor in the analysis of the dominance and variety of languages in international communication.

5. *International scientific publications:* International scientific publications, both online and print, contain the languages of global intellectual discourse, thus critically impacting intellectual communities involved in the production, reproduction, and circulation of knowledge around the world.

Given these highly complex interactions, research in this area frequently yields contradictory conclusions. Unable to reach a general agreement, experts in the field have developed several different hypotheses. One model posits a clear correlation between the growing global significance of a few languages—particularly English, Chinese, and Spanish—and the declining number of other languages around the world. Another model suggests that the globalization of language does not necessarily mean that our descendants are destined to utilize only a few tongues. Still another thesis emphasizes the power of the Anglo-American culture industry to make English—or what some commentators call 'Globish'—*the* global lingua franca of the 21st century.

To be sure, the rising significance of the English language has a long history, reaching back to the birth of British colonialism in the late 16th century. At that time, only approximately 7 million people used English as their mother tongue. By the 1990s, this number had swollen to over 350 million native speakers, with 400 million more using English as a second language. Almost half of the world's growing population of foreign students is enrolled at institutions in Anglo-American countries. In 2021, more than 60 per cent of the content posted at the top 100 million websites on the World Wide Web (out of a total of 1.9 billion) was in English; only 1.4 per cent was in Chinese.

At the same time, however, the number of spoken languages in the world has dropped from about 14,500 in 1500 to about 6,700 in 2000 (see Table 3). By the end of the second decade of the 21st century, this number had dropped to 6,300, with 2,000 of those languages spoken by fewer than 1,000 people. Given the current rate of decline, some linguists predict that 50–90 per cent of the currently existing languages will have disappeared by the end of the 21st century. But the world's languages are not the only entities threatened with extinction. The spread of consumerist values and materialist lifestyles has endangered the ecological health of our planet as well. It is to this crucial ecological dimension of globalization we now must turn.

Table 3. The declining number of languages around the world, 1500s–2000s

Continents	Early 16th Century	Early 17th Century	Early 18th Century	Early 19th Century	Early 20th Century	Early 21st Century
Americas	2,175	2,025	1,800	1,500	1,125	1,005
Africa	4,350	4,050	3,600	3,000	2,250	2,011
Europe	435	405	360	300	225	201
Asia	4,785	4,455	3,960	3,300	2,475	2,212
Pacific	2,755	2,565	2,280	1,900	1,425	1,274
World	14,500	13,500	12,000	10,000	7,500	6,703

Chapter 6
The ecological dimension of globalization

Although we have examined the economic, political, and cultural aspects of globalization separately, it is important to remember that each of these dimensions impacts the other domains. Nowhere is this more clearly demonstrated than in the ecological dimension of globalization. In recent years, global environmental issues such as global climate change and transboundary pollution have received enormous attention from research institutes, the media, politicians, economists, and the public in general. Unsustainable forms of *ecological globalization* are now recognized as threatening all life on our planet. The worldwide impacts of natural and man-made disasters—such as the horrifying 1986 nuclear plant accident at Chernobyl, Ukraine, the massive 2010 Deepwater Horizon oil spill in the Gulf of Mexico, and the nuclear plant spill at Fukushima, Japan, in 2011—clearly show that the formidable environmental problems of our time can only be tackled by a global alliance of states and civil society actors.

In the 21st century, it has become virtually impossible to ignore the fact that people everywhere on our planet are inextricably linked to each other through the air they breathe, the climate they depend upon, the food they eat, and the water they drink. In spite of this obvious lesson of interdependence, our planet's ecosystems are subjected to continuous human assault in order to maintain wasteful lifestyles. Indeed, a growing number of scientists who recognize the extended scope of recent global change argue that we now live in the *Anthropocene*. This concept refers to the present geological age during which our species has become a major geophysical agent affecting Earth's climate and environment in unprecedented ways.

Cultural values greatly influence how people view their natural environment. For example, cultures steeped in Taoist, Buddhist, and various animist religions often emphasize the interdependence of all living beings—even if their adapted capitalist practices do not always live up to their cultural imperative of maintaining a delicate balance between human wants and ecological needs. Judaeo-Christian humanism contains deeply dualistic values that put humans in control of nature. In Western modernity, the environment has thus come to be considered as a 'resource' to be used instrumentally to fulfil the needs and desires of human 'consumers'. Consider, for example, the cutting down of rainforests around the world in the name of 'harvesting resources'. It threatens the livelihood and cultures of indigenous people, not to speak of the countless animal and plant species that have been wiped out merely to serve oversized human

The Anthropocene framework

The Anthropocene framework allows for deeper reflections on the current dynamics of ecological globalization across a broader range of spatial scales and trajectories. It gives us a more accurate picture of Earth as a complex system that is constantly reacting to problems posed by the imbalance of the forces and flows of which it is composed. The Anthropocene framework also serves the important purpose of conceiving of human existence and social change in the context of the perpetual transformation of our home planet. Hence, our attention to the Earth's vast ecosystems requires a good understanding of the social processes that go by the name of globalization.

demands. Still, the capitalist culture industry seeks to convince its global audience that the meaning and chief value of life can be found in the limitless accumulation of material goods.

One major environmental concern relates to still uncontrolled population growth in parts of the global South and the lavish consumption patterns in the global North. Since farming economies first came into existence about 480 generations ago, the world population has exploded a thousand-fold to reach nearly 7.8 billion in 2022. Half of this increase has occurred in since the 1990s. With the possible exception of rats and mice, humans are now the most numerous mammals on earth. Vastly increased demands for food, timber, and fibre have put severe pressure on the planet's ecosystems.

Large areas of the Earth's surface, especially in arid and semi-arid regions, have been used for agricultural production for millennia, yielding crops for ever-increasing numbers of people. Concerns about the relationship between population growth and environmental degradation are frequently focused rather narrowly on aggregate population levels. Yet, the global impact of humans on the environment is as much a function of per capita consumption as it is of overall population size (see Table 4). For example, the United States comprises only 6 per cent of the world's population, yet it consumes 30–40 per cent of our planet's natural resources. Together, regional overconsumption and uncontrolled population growth present a serious problem to the health of our planet. Unless we are willing to rethink the relentless drive for profits-at-all-cost that sustains these ominous dynamics, the health of Mother Earth is likely to deteriorate further.

Some of the effects of overconsumption and population growth are painfully obvious in the recurrent food crises plaguing vast regions of our planet. Large-scale food riots in Haiti, Indonesia, the Philippines, China, Cameroon, and South Sudan in the 21st century highlight increasing limitations on access to food in

Table 4. Annual consumption patterns (per capita) in selected countries, 2017–22

	Annual oil consumption per capita (in litres)	Automobiles per 1,000 people	Annual meat consumption per capita (in kg)	Annual use of fresh water per capita (in litres)
US	3,556	837	124	3,794
South Korea	2,834	485	70	1,643
France	1,525	667	83	1,244
Brazil	832	366	100	844
Egypt	559	70	26	2,202
China	525	219	61	1,165
Burundi	8	10	12	124

part as a result of environmental problems such as drought. Other factors include rising oil prices (which affect the cost of transportation of food), diversion of food staples such as corn into production of biofuels in efforts to reduce reliance on petroleum, and unequal access to resources across developed and developing countries. The problem of adequate food supply for so many people highlights the interconnections between political, economic, and ecological problems that are accentuated by the process of globalization.

Another significant ecological problem associated with population increases and the globalization of environmental degradation is the worldwide *reduction of biodiversity* (see Figure F). Many biologists today believe that the world is now in the midst of the fastest mass extinction of living species in the 4.5-billion-year history of the

F. Major manifestations and consequences of global environmental degradation.

planet. According to OECD reports, two-thirds of the world's farmlands have been rated as 'somewhat degraded' and one-third have been marked as 'strongly degraded'. More than half the world's wetlands have already been destroyed, and the biodiversity of freshwater ecosystems is under serious threat. Three-quarters of worldwide genetic diversity in agricultural crop and animal breeds has been lost since 1900. Some experts fear that up to 50 per cent of all plant and animal species—most of them in the global South—will disappear by the end of this century. Hence, many environmentalists argue that biodiversity should be treated as a planetary asset and held in trust for the benefit of future generations.

Some of the measures currently undertaken to safeguard biodiversity include the creation of hundreds of *gene banks* located in over 100 countries around the world. One of the most spectacular of these banks is the Svalbard Global Seed Vault buried in permafrost in a mountain on the Arctic island of Spitzbergen. Officially opened in 2008, this 'Doomsday Vault' was funded by the Global Crop Diversity Trust (financed by international donors like the Gates and Rockefeller Foundations) and specially designed to store back-up copies of the seeds of the world's major food crops at −18°C. Operating like a safety deposit box in a bank, the Global Seed Vault is free of charge to public and private depositors and kept safe by the Norwegian government. But it is doubtful that such laudable back-up measures are sufficient to reverse the escalating loss of biodiversity brought about by humanity's ecological footprint.

Transboundary pollution represents another grave danger to our collective survival. The release of vast amounts of synthetic chemicals into the air and water has created conditions for human and animal life that are outside previous limits of biological experience. For example, chlorofluorocarbons (CFCs) were used in the second half of the 20th century as non-flammable refrigerants, industrial solvents, foaming agents, and aerosol propellants. In the mid-1970s, researchers noted that the unregulated release of

CFCs into the air seemed to be depleting Earth's protective ozone layer. A decade later, the discovery of large 'ozone holes' over Tasmania, New Zealand, and large parts of the Antarctic finally resulted in a coordinated international effort to phase out production of CFCs and other ozone-depleting substances. Scientists have warned that the risk of damage to the world's ozone layer has increased as a result of more frequent and severe storms and other extreme weather events associated with global climate change. Other forms of transboundary pollution include industrial emissions of sulphur and nitrogen oxides. Returning to the ground in the form of acid rain, these chemicals damage forests, soils, and freshwater ecosystems. Current acid deposits in northern Europe and parts of North America are far higher than the tolerable range suggested by environmental agencies.

Finally, the ominous phenomenon of *human-induced climate change* has emerged as *the* major focus of domestic and intergovernmental policy as well as grass roots activism. Brought to wider public attention by former US Vice President Al Gore in the 2000s through his award-winning documentary *An Inconvenient Truth*—as well as the production of numerous scientific reports outlining the dire consequences of unchecked global warming—climate change is clearly one of the top global problems facing humanity today (see Figure 12).

But perhaps the most influential recent attempt to raise people's consciousness about the dangers of global climate change came from an unexpected quarter: the Vatican in Rome. In September 2015, Pope Francis I stood before the UN General Assembly and issued a radical call for the world to address global warming (see Figure 13). Connecting the issue of climate change to the wider pursuit of equality, security, and social justice, the pontiff went so far as to send his shoes to the 2015 UNIPCC Climate Summit in Paris, to be displayed at the city's Place de la République together with thousands of shoes of other climate-change protesters as a public symbol to curb carbon emissions.

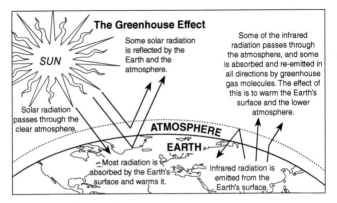

12. The greenhouse effect.

Pope Francis's climate appeal

'I urgently appeal, then, for a new dialogue about how we are shaping the future of our planet. We need a conversation which includes everyone, since the environmental challenge we are undergoing, and its human roots, concern and affect us all. The worldwide ecological movement has already made considerable progress and led to the establishment of numerous organizations committed to raising awareness of these challenges. Regrettably, many efforts to seek concrete solutions to the environmental crisis have proved ineffective, not only because of powerful opposition but also because of a more general lack of interest. Obstructionist attitudes, even on the part of believers, can range from denial of the problem to indifference, nonchalant resignation or blind confidence in technical solutions. We require a new and universal solidarity.'

13. Pope Francis I addresses the UN General Assembly on climate change, 25 September 2015.

The consequences of worldwide climate change, especially global warming, could be catastrophic. A large number of scientists are calling for concerted action by governments to curb greenhouse gas emissions. Indeed, global warming represents a grim exampleof the decisive shift in both the intensity and extent of contemporary environmental problems. The rapid build-up of gas emissions, including carbon dioxide, methane, nitrous and sulphur oxides, and CFCs, in our planet's atmosphere has greatly enhanced Earth's capacity to trap heat. The resulting *greenhouse effect* is responsible for raising average temperatures worldwide.

The precise effects of global warming are difficult to calculate. According to three recent reports by the United Nations Intergovernmental Panel on Climate Change (IPCC) issued between 2018 and 2022, the world was 1°C above pre-industrial levels in 2017. It is now heading towards 1.5°C within a decade or so. The *high confidence* range predicted for this threshold is between 2030 and 2040. At more than 2°C global warming, it has been suggested that the world will descend towards ecological chaos, with the most severe impacts hitting the equatorial regions. To give some sense of the difference between these two apparently close thresholds: at 1.5°C, the IPCC estimates that around 80 per cent of coral reefs will be gone; at 2°C, they will be 99 per cent destroyed. Higher temperatures are already worsening many kinds of extreme weather events, including storms, wildfires, floods, and droughts. Nine of the 10 warmest years have occurred since 2005, with the 5 hottest happening since 2017. Disasters caused by global climate change not only endanger human lives, but cause trillions of dollars of damage.

These significant increases in global temperatures have also led to meltdowns of large chunks of the world's major ice reserves. The polar ice caps have melted faster in the last few decades than in the last 10,000. The large Greenland ice sheet is shrinking the fastest, and its complete melting would result in a global rise of sea levels of up to 22 feet. However, even a much smaller sea level rise would spell doom for many coastal regions around the world. The small Pacific island nations of Tuvalu and Kiribati, for example, would disappear. Large coastal cities such as Tokyo, New York, London, and Sydney would lose significant chunks of their urban landscapes.

But sea level and water temperature rise as a result of global warming are not the only serious problems threatening the health of our planet's oceans. Overfishing, the loss of coral reefs, coastal pollution, acidification, mega-oil spills, and illegal dumping of hazardous wastes have had a devastating impact on Earth's marine environments. Consider, for example, the *Great Pacific Garbage Patch*—a gigantic floating mass of often toxic, non-biodegradable plastics and chemical sludge twice the size of Texas that circulates permanently in the powerful currents of the Northern Pacific Ocean.

Or, perhaps even more horrifying, take the huge floating debris field generated by the devastating Japanese earthquake and tsunami of March 2011 that killed more than 15,000 people across Japan. The disaster caused the partial destruction of the Fukushima Daiichi nuclear plant, in the process allowing the escape of harmful radioactive particles into air and water. Stretching for nearly 2,000 miles and still containing 1.5 million tonnes of detritus (3.5 million tonnes have already sunk), this debris field crossed the Pacific in only 15 months. It deposited on North America's Pacific coast massive amounts of partially toxic materials such as wall insulation, oil and gas canisters, car tyres, fishing nets, and Styrofoam buoys. Heavier items are drifting underwater and might wash up in years to come.

The central feature of all these potentially disastrous environmental problems is that they are *glocal*, thus making them serious problems for all sentient beings inhabiting our magnificent blue planet. The dark side of unchecked environmental glocalization became especially visible in the estimated 11,264 bushfires in Australia that burnt 13 million acres between July 2019 and February 2020; 58,985 wildfires affecting 7.1 million acres in the US in 2021; and the 87,000 wildfires raging in the Amazon region of Brazil in the summer of 2019. Encouraged by the anti-ecological views of the country's national-populist President Jair Bolsonaro, scores of Brazilian ranchers and farmers had intentionally set many of those fires to clear heavily forested land for agricultural purposes. As French President Emmanuel Macron pointed out, these local burnings had serious global consequences. After all, the Amazonian rainforests serve as the world's 'lungs' by producing 20 per cent of our planet's oxygen. Indeed, transboundary pollution, global warming, climate change, and species extinction are challenges that cannot be contained within national or even regional borders. They do not have isolated causes and effects, for they are caused by aggregate collective human actions and thus require a coordinated global response.

To be sure, ecological problems aggravated by globalization also have significant economic ramifications. Although these effects will be more significant for less developed countries than for rich countries, they will nonetheless affect all people and all nations. Poor countries do not have the necessary infrastructure or income to adapt to the unavoidable climate changes that will occur because of carbon emissions already in the earth's atmosphere. As we noted, developing regions are already warmer on average than most developed countries and consequently suffer from a high degree of variability in rainfall. To make matters worse, less developed countries are also heavily dependent on agriculture for the majority of their income. Since agriculture is the most climate sensitive of all economic sectors, developing nations will be more adversely affected by climate change than developed countries.

Further consequences of this vicious circle include increased illnesses, escalating death rates, and crumbling infrastructure. The cost of living will continue to rise, leaving poor households and communities unable to save for future emergencies. Recent scientific reviews explicitly link the problem of climate change to development and aid provision in poor countries. They will require assistance from the developed world if they are to adapt and survive climate change. Thus, climate change and global warming are not merely environmental or scientific issues. They are economic, political, cultural, but, above all, ethical issues that have been expanded and intensified by the process of globalization.

There has been much debate in public and academic circles about the severity of climate change and the best ways for the global community to respond to it. As can be gleaned from the list of major global environmental treaties, international discussion on the issue of global warming and environmental degradation has been occurring for over 30 years. Yet, while much has been written and spoken about this issue, few coordinated measures have been implemented. Most international environmental treaties still lack effective enforcement mechanisms.

For the most part, political efforts in favour of immediate change have been limited. Even the most significant international accord, struck in December 2015 at the UN Framework Convention on Climate Change summit held in Paris, France, turned out to be less durable than expected when then President Trump removed his country from the treaty. In the wake of this decision, other governments decided to water down or postpone some key elements of the *Paris global climate deal* agreed to by all parties.

Even the 2021 UN Climate Change Conference in Glasgow, Scotland—with the new US government of President Biden having rejoined the climate accord and fully represented at the meeting—achieved only moderate outcomes that were greeted by most environmentalists as a great disappointment (see Table 5).

Six Key elements of the 2015 Paris climate deal

1. Limit global temperature rises to below 2 degrees Celsius.

2. Reach global peaking of global greenhouse gas emissions (GHGs) as soon as possible and develop concrete GHGs reduction targets.

3. Enhance adaptive capacity, strengthen resilience, and reduce vulnerability to climate change.

4. Pursue domestic legislation to achieve these three goals.

5. Developed countries have an obligation to support the efforts of developing countries to build clean, climate-resilient futures and provide resources to that end.

6. Enhance climate change education, training, and public awareness.

Table 5. Major global environmental treaties/conferences, 1972–2021

Name of Treaty/Conference	Coverage/protection	Date
UNESCO-World Heritage, Paris	Cultural and natural heritage	1972
UNEP Conference, Stockholm	General environment	1972
CITES, Washington, DC	Endangered species	1973
Marine pollution treaty, London	Marine pollution from ships	1978
UN Convention on Law of the Sea	Marine species, pollution	1982
Vienna Protocol	Ozone layer	1985
Montreal Protocol	Ozone layer	1987
Basel Convention	Hazardous wastes	1989
UN 'Rio Summit' on Environmental Climate Change	Biodiversity	1992
Jakarta Mandate	Marine and coastal diversity	1995
Kyoto Protocol	Global warming	1997
Rotterdam Convention	Industrial pollution	1998
Johannesburg World Summit	Ecological sustainability, pollution	2002
Bali Action Plan	Global warming	2007
UN Copenhagen Climate Summit	Global warming	2009
UN Cancun Climate Summit	Global warming	2010
UN Durban Climate Summit	Global warming	2011
UN Rio + 20	Sustainable development	2012
UN Paris Climate Summit	Climate change	2015
UN Glasgow Climate Summit	Climate change	2021

Much depends on whether major countries are willing to redouble their efforts in taking more serious steps in the direction of global environmental sustainability. Growing numbers of ordinary citizens—often led by a new generation of global environmental activists like Greta Thunberg—demand resolute government action in favour of environmental regulations, reduced emission standards, and a switch from fossil fuels to renewable energy sources such as solar, wind, and wave as soon as possible (see Tables 6 and 7). Humanity was afforded a good glimpse of what an ecologically more sustainable future might look like when the COVID-19 pandemic caused multiple global lockdowns in 2020/1. Satellite images showed that within weeks, the skies over heavily polluted global cities like Beijing, Delhi, and Cairo began to clear up. Not only did air and water pollution decrease, but the reduced human impact on the environment also boosted wildlife, including

Table 6. The top-10 carbon dioxide emitters, 2020

Country	Total emissions (million tonnes of CO_2)	Per capita emissions (tonnes per capita)
People's Republic of China	11,680	8.2
United States of America	4,535	13.7
India	2,411	1.7
Russian Federation	1,674	11.6
Japan	1,067	8.3
Islamic Republic of Iran	690	8.3
Germany	636	7.7
South Korea	621	12.1
Saudi Arabia	589	16.7
Indonesia	568	2.1
Global total	36,153	4.7

Table 7. Long-term global CO$_2$ emissions, 1750–2020

Year	Million metric tonnes of carbon
1750	3
1800	8
1850	54
1900	534
1950	1,630
2000	23,650
2020	37,000

endangered species. Indeed, many commentators observed that such an 'anthropo-pause', however tragic and unintended, impressed on billions of people the urgency of finding alternative paths of ecological globalization.

The growing public debate over climate change serves as another instructive example for how the major dimensions of globalization intersect. In this case, political and economic globalization simply has not kept up with the ecological demands of our planet. But time is of the essence. Some leading scientists believe that a further decade or two of slow or no action would make it too late to reverse the disastrous course of climate change and ecological degradation. It now has become abundantly clear to many people that the contemporary period of the Anthropocene has been the most environmentally destructive period in human history. It remains to be seen, however, whether the growing recognition of the ecological limits of our planet will translate swiftly into profound new forms of political cooperation across borders. As we shall discuss in Chapter 7, the current ideological clashes over the meaning and direction of globalization play a major role in the global struggle over the fate of our wondrous planet.

Chapter 7
Ideological confrontations over globalization

Like all social processes, globalization operates in an *ideological* dimension filled with potent narratives and discourses about the phenomenon itself—such as the heated public debate over whether globalization should be seen as 'good' or 'bad'. *Ideologies* are powerful systems of widely shared ideas, patterned beliefs, and strong emotions. Accepted as truth by significant groups in society, these shared mental maps offer people a more or less coherent picture of the world not only as it is, but also how it ought to be. In doing so, they help organize the tremendous complexity of human experiences into fairly simple claims that serve as guide and compass for social and political action. These claims are employed by social elites to legitimize their interests and to defend or challenge existing power structures.

Contrary to the notion of an 'end of ideology' that gained much popularity at the closing of the Cold War, the early 21st century has witnessed fierce *ideological confrontations* between various globalisms. *Market globalism* still operates as the dominant ideology which seeks to endow 'globalization' with neoliberal meanings. Contesting it from the political Left, *justice globalism* constructs an alternative vision of globalization based on egalitarian ideals of global solidarity and distributive justice. From the political Right, *religious globalism* struggles against both market globalism and justice globalism as it seeks to bring about a religious community. In spite of their considerable differences, however, these three globalisms share an important function discussed in Chapter 1: they articulate the rising global imaginary in competing political programmes and agendas.

These conflicting globalization narratives have been confronted by *anti-globalists* such as Donald Trump in the US, Marine Le Pen in France, and Nigel Farage in the UK. Clinging to the national imaginary of the past, these *national-populists* have made much headway in challenging the ideological dominance of market globalism. Their political vision reflects their fierce opposition to the transnational dynamics at the core of globalization. Let us briefly examine each of these influential ideologies in turn.

Market globalism

During the 1990s, market globalism was codified and disseminated worldwide by global power elites that included corporate managers, executives of large transnational corporations, corporate lobbyists, influential journalists and public-relations specialists, public intellectuals, celebrities and entertainers, state bureaucrats, and politicians. Serving as the chief advocates of market globalism, these market globalists saturated the public discourse with neoliberal images of a consumerist world. Selling their preferred version of a single global marketplace to the public, they portrayed globalization in a positive light as an indispensable tool for the realization of a better global order.

Such favourable visions of globalization as benign market integration still shape public opinion and political choices in many parts of the world. Given that the exchange of commodities constitutes one of the core activities of all societies, the market-oriented discourse of globalization itself has turned into an extremely important commodity destined for public consumption. *Business Week*, *The Economist*, *Forbes*, the *Wall*

Street Journal, and the *Financial Times* are among the most powerful of dozens of electronic media published globally that feed their readers a steady diet of market globalist claims. The constant repetition of these slogans has the capacity to (re) produce what they name. As more neoliberal policies are enacted, the claims of market globalism become even more firmly planted in the public mind.

An analysis of hundreds of newspaper and magazine articles—both online and offline—yields five major ideological claims that occur with great regularity in the utterances, speeches, and writings of influential market globalists.

Like all ideologies, market globalism starts with the attempt to establish an authoritative definition of its core concept. As we observed in Chapter 3, such an account is anchored in the neoliberal idea of the self-regulating market that serves as the framework for a future global order. But the problem with Claim 1 is that its core message of liberalizing and integrating markets is only realizable through the *political* project of engineering free markets. Thus, market globalists have utilized the *powers of government* to weaken and eliminate those social policies and institutions that curtail the market. Such actions, however, stand in stark contrast to the neoliberal idealization of the limited role of government.

The five claims of market globalism

1. Globalization is about the liberalization and global integration of markets.
2. Globalization is inevitable and irreversible.
3. Nobody is in charge of globalization.
4. Globalization benefits everyone.
5. Globalization furthers the spread of democracy in the world.

Claim 2 establishes the historical inevitability and irreversibility of globalization understood as the liberalization and global integration of markets. The portrayal of globalization as some sort of natural force, like the weather or gravity, makes it easier for market globalists to convince people that they must adapt to the discipline of the market if they are to survive and prosper. Hence, the claim of inevitability seeks to depoliticize the public discourse about globalization. Neoliberal policies are portrayed to be above politics; they simply carry out what is ordained by nature. However, as we shall see below, former British Prime Minister Margaret Thatcher's quip that 'there is no alternative' has been belied by the emergence of justice globalism.

Market globalism's deterministic language offers yet another rhetorical advantage. If the natural laws of the market have indeed preordained a neoliberal course of history, then globalization does not reflect the arbitrary agenda of a particular social class or group. In that case, market globalists merely carry out the unalterable imperatives of a benign transcendental force. People aren't in charge of globalization, markets and technology are. But those voices behind Claim 3 are right only in a formal sense. While there is no conscious conspiracy orchestrated by a single, evil force, this does not mean that nobody is in charge of globalization. It is the market globalist initiative to integrate and deregulate markets around the world that both creates and sustains asymmetrical power relations.

Claim 4—globalization benefits everyone—lies at the very core of market globalism because it provides an affirmative answer to the crucial normative question of whether globalization should be considered a 'good' or a 'bad' thing. But when market dynamics dominate social and political outcomes, the opportunities and rewards of globalization are spread often unequally, concentrating power and wealth amongst a select group of people, regions, and corporations at the expense of the multitude.

Claim 5—globalization furthers the spread of democracy in the world—is rooted in the neoliberal assertion that free markets and democracy are synonymous terms. Persistently affirmed as 'common sense', the actual compatibility of these concepts often goes unchallenged in the public discourse. Indeed, this claim hinges on a conception of democracy that emphasizes formal procedures such as voting at the expense of the direct participation of broad majorities in political and economic decision-making. Hence, the assertion that globalization furthers the spread of democracy in the world is largely based on a rather thin definition of democracy.

Our examination of the five central claims of market globalism suggests that the neoliberal language about globalization is ideological in the sense that it is politically motivated and contributes toward the construction of particular meanings of globalization that preserve and stabilize existing power relations. Market globalism employs powerful narratives that sell an overarching neoliberal worldview, thereby creating collective meanings and shaping people's identities. Over the last two decades, however, massive justice-globalist protests and jihadist-globalist acts of terrorism are clear evidence for the fact that market globalism has encountered ideological resistance.

Justice globalism

Justice globalism refers to the political ideas and values associated with the social alliances and political actors known as the 'global justice movement' (GJM). It emerged in the 1990s as a progressive network of international NGOs and activist groups, defined in Chapter 4 as a 'global civil society'. Dedicated to the establishment of a more equitable relationship between the global North and South, the GJM agitated for the protection of the global environment, fair trade and international labour issues, human rights, and women's issues. As the 20th century drew to a close, the ideological contest between market globalism and its emerging challenger on the political Left erupted in street protests in many cities around the world. At the famous 'Battle of Seattle', for example, tens of thousands of citizens demonstrated against the neoliberal policies of the WTO (see Figure 14).

In the first decade of the 21st century, the forces of justice globalism maintained their political pressure. This was evidenced by the emergence of the World Social Forum (WSF), which serves as *the* key ideological site of justice globalism. The WSF was deliberately set up as a 'shadow organization' to the market globalist World Economic Forum (WEF) in Davos, Switzerland. Its annual meetings in the global South draw tens of thousands of delegates from around the world. Just like market globalists who treated the WEF as a platform to project their ideas and claims to a global audience, justice globalists utilized the WSF to publicize their policy demands for a *new global deal*.

14. Police confronting WTO protesters in downtown Seattle, 30 November 1999.

From the WSF Charter of Principles

1. The World Social Forum is an open meeting place for reflective thinking, democratic debate of ideas, formulation of proposals, free exchange of experiences, and interlinking for effective action by groups and movements of civil society that are opposed to neoliberalism and to domination of the world by capital and any form of imperialism and are committed to building a planetary society directed toward fruitful relationships among humankind and between it and the Earth...8. The World Social Forum is a plural, diversified, confessional, nongovernmental, and non-party context that, in a decentralized fashion, interrelates organizations and movements engaged in concrete action at levels from the local to the international to build another world...13. As a context for interrelations, the World Social Forum seeks to strengthen and create new national and international links among organizations and movement of society that—in both public and private life—will increase the capacity for non-violent social resistance to the process of dehumanization the world is undergoing...

In the wake of the 2008 GFC, various 'Occupy' movements around the world became the new face of justice globalism. In the US, Occupy Wall Street (OWS) burst onto the political scene in 2011 as part of a global protest movement that drew activists into the world's major cities within months. Inspired by the popular Arab Spring protests in the Middle East and the *Los Indignados* demonstrations in Spain, Occupy activists expressed outrage at the inequalities of globalization that enriched the '1 per cent' at the expense of the '99 per cent'. Occupy protesters across the world gathered at spaces of symbolic importance—such as New York City's Zuccotti Park near Wall Street—and sought to create, in miniature, the kind of egalitarian society they wanted to live in. Rejecting conventional organizational leadership formations, OWS formed decentralized 'General Assemblies' and working groups. However, their efforts to reach decisions through a consensus-based process turned out to be politically ineffective—a major factor in the relatively quick dissipation of the Occupy movement.

Challenging the central claims of market globalism, justice globalists believe that *another world is possible*, as the WSF's principal slogan suggests. Envisioning the construction of a new world order based on a global redistribution of wealth and power, they emphasize the crucial connection between globalization and local wellbeing. Justice globalists accuse market globalist elites of pushing neoliberal policies that are leading to greater global inequality, high levels of unemployment, environmental degradation, and the demise of social welfare. Over the last two decades, justice globalists have formulated five central ideological claims in opposition to the 'corporate agenda' of market globalists.

Global New Deal: five demands

1. A global 'Marshall Plan' that includes a blanket forgiveness of all Third World Debt;
2. Levying of the so-called 'Tobin Tax': a tax on international financial transactions that would benefit the global South;
3. Abolition of offshore financial centres that offer tax havens for wealthy individuals and corporations;
4. Implementation of stringent global environmental agreements;
5. Implementation of a more equitable global development agenda.

Religious globalisms

As justice globalists organized demonstrations against the IMF and World Bank, Al Qaeda terrorists struck the US on 11 September 2001. Nearly 3,000 innocent people from many countries perished in less than two hours, including hundreds of heroic NYC police and firefighters trapped in the collapsing towers of the World Trade Center (see Figure 15). In the years following the 9/11 attacks, it became clear that Islamist extremists were not confining their terrorist activities to the United States. Regional jihadist networks like ISIS, Al Qaeda, Jemaah Islamiya, Boko Haram, Al Shabaab, and Abu Sayyaf regularly targeted civilians and military personnel around the globe.

ISIS and Al Qaeda remain even in the 2020s two extremely violent Islamic examples of organizations that subscribe to religious globalism. Other religiously inspired visions of a global political community united by faith have been espoused by fundamentalist Christian groups such as the Army of God and Christian Identity, the Mormon Church, the Falun Gong sect, the Aum Shinrikyo cult, and Chabad, an orthodox Jewish movement with global ambitions. This is not to suggest that *all* religiously inspired articulations of a global community are conservative, reactionary, or violent. A key

15. The burning twin towers of the World Trade Center,
11 September 2001.

point about the religious globalisms, however, is that these ideologies aim at global hegemony and demand to be given primacy and superiority over state-based and secular political structures. In some cases, like ISIS or Aum Shinrikyo, they are prepared to use extremely violent means—often couched in terms like a 'cosmic war'—to achieve their end goal.

While jihadist Islamism is today's most spectacular manifestation of religious globalism, it would be a mistake to equate the ideology of ISIS or Al Qaeda with the religion of Islam or even more peaceful strands of 'political Islam' or 'Islamist fundamentalism'. Rather, the term 'jihadist Islamism' is meant to apply to those extremely violent strains of Islam-influenced ideologies that place a religiously inspired warfare at the heart of their belief. As the terrorist activities of ISIS or Boko Haram have shown, jihadist Islamism is the most influential and successful attempt yet to articulate the rising global imaginary into a religious globalism.

Jihadist Islamism is anchored in the core concepts of *umma* (Islamic community of believers) and *jihad* (both armed and unarmed struggle against unbelief purely for the sake of God and his *umma*). Indeed, jihadist globalists understand the *umma* as a single community of believers united in their belief in the one and only God. Expressing a religious-populist yearning for strong leaders who set things right by fighting alien invaders and corrupt Islamic elites, they claim to return power back to the 'Muslim masses' and restore the *umma* to its earlier glory. In their view, the process of regeneration must start with a small but dedicated vanguard of religious warriors willing to sacrifice their lives as martyrs to the holy cause of awakening people to their sacred duties—not just in traditionally Islamic countries, but wherever members of the *umma* yearn for the necessary establishment of God's rule on earth.

With a third of the world's Muslims living today as minorities in non-Islamic countries, jihadist Islamists regard the restoration as no longer a local, national, or even regional event. Rather, it requires a concerted *global* effort spearheaded by jihadists operating in various localities around the world. Indeed, this form of religious globalism holds special appeal for Muslim youths between the ages of 15 and 30 who have lived for sustained periods of time in the individualized and deculturated environments of Westernized Islam. This new wave of jihadist recruits, responsible for some of the most spectacular terrorist operations of the last two decades, were products of a Westernized Islam.

Thus, jihadist globalism takes place in a global space emancipated from the confining territoriality of 'Syria', or the 'Middle East' that used to constitute the political framework of religious nationalists fighting modern secular regimes in the 20th century. Although organizations like ISIS embrace the Manichean dualism of a 'clash of civilizations' between their imagined *umma* and 'global unbelief', their globalist ideology clearly transcends clear-cut civilizational fault lines. While jihadist Islamism still retains potent metaphors that resonate with people's national or even tribal solidarities, its chilling vision contains an ideological alternative to both market globalism and justice globalism that imagines community in unambiguously global terms.

The challenge of antiglobalist populism

The dire economic consequences of the GFC and the ensuing Great Recession were amplified by the willingness to support harsh austerity policies that hit ordinary people hard as well as the failure of the neoliberal establishment to punish the financial sector for its economic irresponsibility. In addition, the perceived threat to traditional cultural identities posed by the enhanced migration flows in the mid-2010s caused a profound shift in the ideological landscape away from the neoliberal vision of a globally integrated world. Ordinary people's belief in the claims of market globalism gave way to widespread fears that the great experiment of transcending the nation-state had spiralled out of control and needed to be curbed. Accusing 'cosmopolitan elites' of cheating the toiling masses, authoritarian politicians soon capitalized on this popular discontent by promising 'the forgotten people' a return to national control. Such calls had already been issued by various European national populists as far back as the 1980s, but had failed to appeal to most voters of conventional mainstream parties.

The full extent of people's anger and resentment towards politics-as-usual was reflected in the unexpected 2016 victory of the pro-Brexit forces in the UK and the stunning election of Donald J. Trump in the United States a few months later. Indeed, the growing power of *right-wing national populism*—and the crucial role played by the digital social media in its meteoric rise—prompted influential media pundits to speak of a *populist explosion*.

What is national populism?

The French philosopher Jean-Pierre Taguieff coined the term *national populism* in 1984 in reference to the political discourse of Jean-Marie Le Pen and his right-wing French political party, *Front National* ('National Front'), renamed in 2018 under the leadership of his daughter Marine Le Pen as *Rassemblement National* ('National Rally'). National populists imagine a mythical national unity based on an essentialized identity linking ethnicity/race and culture. They claim to defend and protect the pure 'common people' against the treachery of 'corrupt elites' and 'parasitical' political institutions. Over the years, a growing number of populism scholars have adopted 'national populism' as an umbrella term for a range of right-wing variants linked to different geographic regions in the world.

But this populist surge did not stop in 2016. For example, national populists consolidated their gains in the 2019 European parliamentary elections. Their parties and candidates vaulted to the top spot not only in their previous strongholds of Hungary and Poland but also in large, traditionally centrist countries such as France and Italy. But the biggest surprise hit the UK where Nigel Farage's newly formed Brexit Party came in first with an astonishing 32 per cent of the vote.

The illiberal and authoritarian leanings of national populism stand in stark contrast to the pluralist and inclusive values of liberal democracy. Yet, populism has been successful in both liberal democracies and authoritarian countries such as Victor Órban's Hungary, Vladimir Putin's Russia, Jair Bolsonaro's Brazil, Norbert Hofer's Austria, Marine Le Pen's France, Matteo Salvini's Italy, Jarosław Kaczyński's Poland, Nigel Farage's United Kingdom, Pauline Hanson's Australia, Iván Duque's Colombia, Rodrigo Duterte's Philippines, and, of course, Donald Trump's United States of America. Even after Trump's defeat in the 2020 election, millions of American nationalist supporters not only refused to believe in the legitimacy of the incoming Biden administration but also thought that the insurgency of 6 January 2021, when pro-Trump crowds stormed the US Capitol, was justified. Hence, it appears that the nationalist backlash against globalization is not a short-term phenomenon but an enduring social dynamic to be reckoned with in the 2020s and beyond.

Mapping Trump's antiglobalist populism

In order to get a better sense of the ideological make-up of national populism, let us examine 'Trumpism' as an example of a particularly potent strain that originated in the political discourse of American national populists like Patrick Buchanan and Ross Perot in the 1990s. These narratives place pejorative meanings of 'globalization' and 'globalism' at their very conceptual core which contrast sharply with sympathies for *economic nationalism*—the view that the economy should be designed in ways that, first and foremost, serve narrow national interests.

Trumpism employs conventional national populist core concepts such as *the pure people* as holders of the *general will* who struggle against *the corrupt elites*. Accused of undermining the will of the people with the help of the corporate media, the 'corrupt establishment' is said to advance their sinister practices of 'selling out the wealth of our nation generated by working people' and filling their own pockets. But Trumpism also links the meaning of 'the elites' to the spectre of 'globalist enemies' working against the interests of the country. Globalists are seen as serving the larger material process of 'globalization', defined by Trump as an elite-engineered project of 'abolishing the nation-state' and creating an international system that functions 'to the detriment of the American worker and the American economy'.

While some of these 'enemies' are explicitly identified as domestic actors such as 'Wall Street bankers' or 'Washington politicians', others are characterized as 'foreign agents'. These include members of the 'international financial elite' as well as entire countries like China, Mexico, and Japan. They are denounced for the alleged misdeeds of 'subsidizing their goods', 'devaluing their currencies', 'violating their agreements', and for 'sending rapists, drug dealers, and other criminals into America'. Indeed, Trump associates globalization with what he calls the 'complete and total disasters' of immigration, crime, and terrorism that are 'destroying our nation'. Immigration, in particular, receives ample treatment in the form of vigorous denunciations of the establishment's 'globalist policies of open borders' that are alleged to endanger the safety and security of the American people.

For Trump, the realization of his central campaign slogan to 'make America great again' requires the systematic separation of the 'national' from the 'global' in all aspects of social life in the US. The

Three central claims of Trump's antiglobalist populism

1. Corrupt elites betray the hardworking American people by shoring up a global order that makes them rich and powerful while compromising the sovereignty and security of the homeland and squandering the wealth of the nation.

2. Americanism, not globalism, will be our credo!

3. The defeat of globalism and its treacherous ideologues will usher in a bright future through the glorious rebirth of the nation.

constant repetition of his nationalist mantra—*Americanism, not globalism, will be our credo*—indicates the enormous significance of globalization in Trump's political discourse. For this reason, it makes sense to refer to this strain of national populism as *antiglobalist populism*. No question, Trump's antiglobalist ideas have produced strong ideological claims that challenge some dominant neoliberal meanings of market globalism.

Ironically, of course, the ubiquitous brand name 'Trump' can hardly be equated with 'Americanism'. Rather it stands for a *global* network of hotels stretching from Honolulu to Rio de Janeiro. Trump's nationalist denunciations of globalization notwithstanding, the towering antiglobalist wave he represents is a globalizing force that has been sweeping across the world. So where is the world going in the 2020s? Let us conclude our discussion with a critical look at the future of globalization in our era of the Great Unsettling—and especially in the context of the protracted COVID-19 pandemic.

Chapter 8
Present and future trends

The magnitude of the global problems and the ensuing massive social changes discussed in this book suggest that globalization might be in real trouble. The global impact of COVID-19 serves as a particularly significant marker of our unsettled times. After all, global interconnectivities and mobilities of various kinds have run up against major pandemic-related obstacles caused by repeated national lockdowns, severe travel restrictions, extended travel quarantines, strict social distancing rules, and a noticeable shift to working-from-home. At the same time, however, both the rapid global spread of COVID-19 and the ensuing global efforts to develop vaccines in record time indicate that certain forms of globalization actually accelerated and intensified during times of worldwide COVID-19-related disruption and paralysis (see Figures G and 16).

Indeed, the development of a safe and highly effective vaccine was the result of a global collaboration between the US-based Pfizer, the world's leading biopharmaceutical company, and BioNTech, a biotechnology company based in Mainz, Germany. These seemingly contradictory dynamics of the breaking and (re)making of worldwide interconnectivities have prompted pundits to raise a crucial question about the future of globalization: are we at the beginning of a 'deglobalization' spiral or are we experiencing a transition to a new 'reglobalization' phase?

As of 20 Jan.: 4   As of 15 Feb.: 28

As of 1 Mar.: 66   As of 20 Mar.: 165

G. Global spread of COVID-19, January–March 2020.

Globalization

16. Empty Leicester Square, West End, London, during a 2020 COVID-19 shutdown.

Deglobalization or reglobalization?

Any attempt to answer this question involves interpretations of vast data sets that have split globalization experts into two antagonistic camps. *Pessimists* posit a *retreat of globalization* measured by its allegedly diminishing component parts. They tend to focus on the economic and political domains such as trade, FDI, and lagging global governance structures. *Optimists*, on the other hand, read the current moment as an *advance of globalization* on the basis of intensifying technological and cultural aspects such as digital flows and cultural mixing. Ironically, these clashing perspectives are presented with complete confidence and certainty that belies our current condition of uncertainty. Both sides cite empirical evidence in support of their respective positions. Breaking the stalemate requires us to move beyond quantitative issues of measurement to a more qualitative re-evaluation of present and future globalization trends.

What we are witnessing is a drastic rearrangement of global dynamics as a result of growing disjunctures and disconnections among the *four principal forms of globalization* we discussed in Chapter 1: embodied globalization, disembodied globalization, objectified globalization, and institutional globalization. While these misalignments have unfolded for a while, they are now being turbocharged by major unsettling events such as the COVID-19 pandemic.

The most consequential movement of disjuncture destabilizing the current globalization system has been occurring between the increasingly digitalized *disembodied form of globalization* and the other three configurations. To put it in a nutshell, the former has been charging ahead while the others have lagged behind—as measured in terms of their extensity, intensity, velocity, and impact. On the surface, this tremendous digital leap pertains to what Klaus Schwab, the Chair of the WEF, has called the 'fourth industrial revolution' or 'Globalization 4.0'.

As noted in Chapter 3, it includes exploding data flows, multiplying computer processing-power, novel digital devices and software packages, the expansion of bandwidth, and the emergence of 5G networks. In communications and data analysis, advanced cloud computing has intersected with machine translation, digitized speech-technologies, artificial intelligence, and machine learning. Global exchange relations have been speeded up through the growth of the platform economy and global commodity-chain management processes, including what has been projected as the Internet of Things. Production has become increasingly automated and trans-spatial through robotics and artificial intelligence. And finance has become one of the drivers of global capitalism, along with derivatives markets that continue to explode. So, too, are intangible assets and the expansion of blockchain technology beyond cryptocurrency—all despite the devasting precedent of the Global Financial Crisis.

Schwab on Globalization 4.0

Globalization 4.0 should begin by accepting that in reality the Fourth Industrial Revolution is more borderless, interconnected, and interdependent than the global economy and integrated supply chains. Second, global cooperation should focus on the governance issues at the heart of the current transformation: cybersecurity, the uses of AI and the gene-editing technology CRISPR, and the intellectual property and data protection agreements. Security, above all, has always been a precondition for globalization. That remains true in cyberspace: when the Internet is not safe, economies suffer. We must ensure the safety of Globalization 4.0's digital sea-lanes and havens.

As the mobility of people, things, and institutions fails to keep up with the broadening of digital networks and the deepening of electronic interconnectivity, the growing stature of disembodied flows in the globalization system begins to scrape off pieces of its adjacent tectonic plates. For example, the application of 3D printing is transforming the global merchandise trade built on global value chains—an aspect of object-related globalization—into regionalized and localized networks of exchange based on digitally enabled production-on-demand as close to the end market as possible. Familiar neoliberal practices of 'outsourcing' and 'offshoring'—hallmarks of object-related globalization—have become destabilized and even reversed as emergent disembodied globalization makes 'reshoring' an attractive option for many companies. Similarly, the service sector is being cannibalized by digital globalization's growing ability to transform embodied workers thousands of miles away into disembodied tele-migrants by means of new collaborative software packages like *Slack* or *Office 365* and electronic project-management platforms like Trello or Basecamp.

It would be a mistake to call this tendency of such turbocharged disembodied globalization to devour its lagging cousins 'deglobalization'. Rather, we are witnessing 'reglobalization', that is, a profound rearrangement of globalization's four major forms, which move at different speeds and at different levels of intensity. To be sure, globalization still entails significant embodied and objectified dynamics, but the story of the present moment is the rising power and significance of its disembodied formation. This understanding of the significance of disjuncture and disunion also enables us to push back much more effectively against the common claim that globalization no longer matters. Typically, such assertions present embodied and objectified globalization such as declining trade and FDI flows as though these were still the dominant dimension and thus represent the sole standards by which to judge the allegedly diminishing significance of globalization in general. In fact, however, globalization still matters a lot—just not in the same way as it did 25 years ago.

To recognize that today's dominant form of globalization is 'disembodied' also opens up new perspectives on changing power relations by bringing into sharper focus novel forms of disembodied power seeking to control and exploit human behaviour. This has been the subject of a landmark study authored by Shoshana Zuboff in 2019. The former Dean of the Harvard Business School describes and analyses practices of Google, Facebook, and Amazon. These corporate digital giants unilaterally claim human experience as free material for translation into behavioural data designed to fuel and shape consumerist desires towards profitable outcomes. Such 'surveillance capitalism' strips away the illusion that the networked form has some kind of indigenous moral content, that being 'connected' is somehow intrinsically pro-social, innately inclusive, or naturally tending toward the democratization of knowledge. Digital connectivity can thus become a mere means to commercial ends: a disembodied

The dark side of Globalization 4.0: Zuboff on *surveillance capitalism*

Surveillance capitalism runs contrary to the early digital dream...Instead, it strips away the illusion that the networked form has some kind of indigenous moral content, that being 'connected' is somehow intrinsically pro-social, innately inclusive, or naturally tending toward the democratization of knowledge. Digital connection is now means to others' commercial ends. At its core, surveillance capitalism is parasitic and self-referential. It revives Karl Marx's old image of capitalism as a vampire that feeds on labour, but with an unexpected turn. Instead of labour, surveillance capitalism feeds on every aspect of the human experience...Google invented and perfected surveillance capitalism...and it quickly spread to Facebook and later Microsoft.

form of power that feeds on every aspect of the embodied human experience.

On a subtler subjective level, the disjunctive movement of globalization—the disproportionate growth of its disembodied formation at the expense of the other configurations—works its way into the subjective sphere of globalization comprising meanings, ideas, moods, sensibilities, and identities. For example, people around the world spend more time in the fluidity and malleability of cyberspace. In 2022, the average American or Briton spent between 43 and 49 hours a week online—up from 9 hours in 2000 (see Figure H). As a result of this advancing process of what has been called *cyberspatiation*, people have become increasingly alienated from the perceived sluggishness and fixity of physical space. They have become aware of the growing disjuncture between their experiences of intensifying global interconnectivity in virtual reality and their existence in the more slowly moving spheres of embodied, objectified, and organizational globalization. This strain produces a divided consciousness torn between their new attachment to the pleasures of digital mobility and their old affection for the social and cultural fixity of familiar local and national life worlds. Thus, people increasingly struggle with heightened sentiments of anxiety, alienation, anomie, and anger. As we have seen in Chapter 7, national-populist politicians, in particular, have benefited from the disjunctive production of the divided consciousness. Experts in using the ideological echo chamber of the global social media have accused footloose 'cosmopolitans' of cheating the toiling masses and reproach the 'liberal media' for spreading 'fake news'. At the same time, however, they rely on the major platforms of digital globalization such as Twitter, Meta, and YouTube. Hence, it is not difficult to see how incongruencies among various globalization flows not only fester political polarization but also lead to cultural resentment and psychological fragmentation.

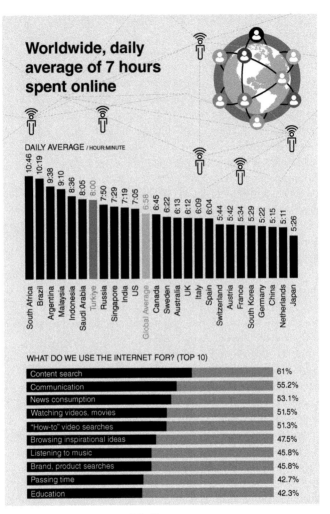

Worldwide, daily average of 7 hours spent online

DAILY AVERAGE / HOUR:MINUTE

South Africa	10:46
Brazil	10:19
Argentina	9:38
Malaysia	9:10
Indonesia	8:36
Saudi Arabia	8:05
Turkiye	8:00
Russia	7:50
Singapore	7:29
India	7:19
US	7:05
Global Average	6:58
Canada	6:45
Sweden	6:22
Australia	6:13
UK	6:12
Italy	6:09
Spain	6:04
Switzerland	5:44
Austria	5:42
France	5:34
South Korea	5:29
Germany	5:22
China	5:15
Netherlands	5:11
Japan	5:26

WHAT DO WE USE THE INTERNET FOR? (TOP 10)

Content search	61%
Communication	55.2%
News consumption	53.1%
Watching videos, movies	51.5%
"How-to" video searches	51.3%
Browsing inspirational ideas	47.5%
Listening to music	45.8%
Brand, product searches	45.8%
Passing time	42.7%
Education	42.3%

H. Daily time spent online globally, 2022.

Towards the future

This rather gloomy assessment of the present informs our brief concluding speculations on how current globalization dynamics might impact future trends. Unfortunately, there seems to be little evidence of impending dramatic reversals. Disjunctive globalization as outlined in this chapter is likely to intensify in this difficult decade of the 2020s. We are now living through the perhaps most visible wave of the Great Unsettling brought on by the COVID-19 pandemic. In spite of mounting problems of cybersecurity and systematic attempts of authoritarian governments to disconnect their citizens from worldwide electronic networks, digital globalization continues to pull even further ahead of its environing formations. COVID-19 has only accelerated these tendencies as schools and universities around the world have made online teaching their default mode of instruction and millions of people have switched to working 'remotely' from their homes. In addition to some perceived benefits such as the elimination of the dreaded commute to work, the materially abstracting effects of globalization's disjunctive dynamics will continue to feed a divided consciousness savouring the glories of the global imaginary yet unwilling to let go of the national imaginary.

Perhaps the most pressing task at hand is deep social reform at the global level with the aim of managing globalization better. Improving globalization depends, in the first instance, on the enhancement of institutional capabilities to make its increasingly complex and disconnected forms work in a more coherent and balanced manner. But even if we confined our efforts to slowing down disembodied globalization and recharging the rest, this task would be immensely difficult. After all, the two main mechanisms required to achieve this goal—the strengthening of global solidarity and the assemblage of more widely shared and effective global governance architecture—are still elusive prospects in our era of the Great Unsettling. The nation-state might be weakening, but the attachment to national interests remains a major driver in the dawning geopolitical order of the 21st century.

But let's end this book on a more optimistic note. The flipside of the apparent degeneration of the current globalization system—experienced as the Great Unsettling—which has been exacerbated by the worldwide spread of COVID-19 and its devastating social impacts—might well be the regeneration of a new and more sustainable globalizing system. Humanity's search for better ways of dealing with global problems can hardly rely on the nationalist reflex to return to an unrecoverable past. Instead, it must draw on a more cosmopolitan spirit that calls for the creation of new global institutions and cooperative networks that would be more attuned to the needs of ordinary people around the world. The emergence of the G20 as a sometimes surprisingly effective deliberative body with the ability to design and coordinate action on a global scale suggests that the idea of global governance is perhaps not as utopian today as it was only a quarter-century ago. Other success stories such as the worldwide reduction of absolute poverty and the formation of an international alliance dedicated to the joint exploration of outer space suggest that the solution to our global problems is not less, but more, and better, globalization.

Without question, the years and decades ahead will bring new global crises and further challenges. Humanity has reached yet another critical juncture—the most significant yet in the relatively short existence of our species. Unless we are willing to let global problems fester to the point where violence and intolerance appear to be the only realistic ways of coping with our unevenly integrating societies, we must link the future course of globalization to the creation of a more just and sustainable world. The necessary transformative social processes must be guided by the polestar of an ethical globalism: the building of a truly democratic and egalitarian global order that protects universal human rights, and our planet, without destroying the biological and cultural diversity that is the lifeblood of human evolution.

References and further reading

There is a great deal of academic literature on globalization, but many of these books are not easily accessible to those who want to acquire some basic knowledge of the subject. Readers who have digested the present volume might find it easier to approach some of the academic works listed here. Some of them have influenced the arguments made in the present volume. Following the overall organization of this book series, however, I have kept direct quotations to a minimum. Still, I wish to acknowledge my intellectual debt to these authors, whose influence on this book is not always obvious from the text.

Chapter 1: What is globalization?

For a better understanding of 'glocalization', consult Victor Roudometof, *Glocalization: A Critical Introduction* (Routledge, 2016).

There are now several excellent academic Global Studies journals dedicated to the study of globalization such as: *Globalizations, Global Networks, New Global Studies,* and *Global Perspectives.*

For an introduction to the transdisciplinary field of global studies, see Manfred B. Steger and Amentahru Wahlrab, *What Is Global Studies? Theory & Practice* (Routledge, 2017); Eve Darian-Smith and Philip McCarthy, *The Global Turn: Theories, Research Designs, and Methods for Global Studies* (University of California Press, 2017); and Mark Juergensmeyer, Saskia Sassen, and Manfred B. Steger, eds, *The Oxford Handbook of Global Studies* (Oxford University Press, 2019).

Matt Stopera's story of his encounter with 'Brother Orange' can be found in 'I followed My Stolen iPhone Across the World, Became a Celebrity in China, and Found a Friend for Life', <https://www.buzzfeed.com/mjs538/i-followed-my-stolen-iphone-across-the-world-became-a-celebr?utm_source=dynamic&utm_campaign=bfshare email>.

Additional short articles on this amazing tale of the lost iPhone include: NPR Staff, 'Buzzfeed Writer's Stolen Phone Sparks Chinese Viral Sensation', <https://www.npr.org/2015/04/02/397096994/buzzfeed-writers-stolen-phone-sparks-chinese-viral-sensation>; and Taylor Lorenz, 'How a man's stolen iPhone made him an internet celebrity in China', <https://www.business insider.com.au/matt-stopera-weibo-celebrity-china-iphone-2015-2>.

The parable of the blind scholars and the elephant most likely originated in the Pali Buddhist Udana, a collection of Buddhist stories compiled in the 2nd century BCE. The many versions of the parable spread to other religions as well, especially to Hinduism and Islam. My thanks go to Professor Ramdas Lamb at the University of Hawai'i at Mānoa for sharing his insightful interpretation of the story.

Chapter 2: Globalization in history

My discussion in the early part of this chapter has greatly benefited from the arguments made by Jared Diamond in his Pulitzer-prizewinning book *Guns, Germs, and Steel* (Norton, 1999). I also recommend two very readable histories of globalization: Nayan Chandra, *Bound Together: How Traders, Preachers, Adventurers, and Warriors Shaped Globalization* (Yale University Press, 2007); and Jeffrey D. Sachs, *The Ages of Globalization: Geography, Technology, and Institutions* (Columbia University Press, 2020).

Accessible books surveying the growing field of global history include: Pamela Kyle Crossley, *What is Global History?* (Polity, 2008); and Sebastian Conrad, *What Is Global History?* (Princeton University Press, 2017).

For a concise explanation of the capitalist world-system, see Immanuel Wallerstein, *World-System Analysis: An Introduction* (Duke University Press, 2004).

The Union of Concerned Scientists is a US-based non-profit organization dedicated to the rigorous practice of independent science to solve our planet's most pressing problems. Its website can be accessed here: <https://www.ucsusa.org/>.

Chapter 3: The economic and technological dimensions of globalization

For the significance of the intensifying interconnectivity between the global economy and digital technology, see Azeem Azhar, *The Exponential Age: How Acceleration Technology is Transforming Business, Politics, and Society* (Diversion Books, 2021). Some data and examples used in this chapter and Chapter 8 have been extracted from this very informative book.

An overview of neoliberalism can be found in Manfred B. Steger and Ravi K. Roy, *Neoliberalism: A Very Short Introduction*, 2nd edn (Oxford University Press, 2021).

The DHL Global Connectedness Index 2021 Update proved to be an excellent empirical source for important economic data and dynamics used in this chapter. It can be accessed here: <https://www.dhl.com/content/dam/dhl/global/dhl-spotlight/documents/pdf/2021-gci-update-report.pdf>.

Additional sources include the annual editions of the UN *Human Development Report* (Oxford University Press), the World Bank's *World Development Report* (Oxford University Press), and the WTO's annual *International Trade Statistics*.

The 2022 Oxfam Report can be accessed at: <https://www.oxfam.org/en/press-releases/pandemic-creates-new-billionaire-every-30-hours-now-million-people-could-fall>.

On the subject of global inequality, see Thomas Piketty, *Capital in the Twenty-First Century* (The Belknap Press, 2014); and Branko Milanovic, *Global Inequality: A New Approach for the Age of Globalization* (The Belknap Press, 2018).

The best short treatment of the 2008 GFC is Robert J. Holton, *Global Finance* (Routledge, 2012). A comprehensive account of the GFC and the ESDC can be found in Adam Tooze, *Crashed: How a Decade of Financial Crises Changed the World* (Viking, 2018).

The 2021 Economic Policy Institute's report, 'CEO pay has skyrocketed 1,322% since 1978' can be accessed here: <https://files.epi.org/uploads/232540.pdf>.

For an accessible summery of the global fiscal response to the COVID-19 pandemic, see Callum Hudson, Benjamin Watson, Alexandra Baker, and Ivailo Arsov, 'The Global Fiscal Response to COVID-19' (2021): <https://www.rba.gov.au/publications/bulletin/2021/jun/pdf/the-global-fiscal-response-to-covid-19.pdf>.

A detailed report on the global economic effects of the coronavirus pandemic issued by the US Congressional Research Service is available at: <https://crsreports.congress.gov/product/pdf/R/R46270/76>.

The 2022 UNCTAD World Investment report can be accessed here: <https://worldinvestmentreport.unctad.org/world-investment-report-2022/>.

Detailed data of the ground-breaking study of TNC networks referred to in this chapter can be found in Stefania Vitali, James B. Glattfelder, and Stefano Battiston, 'The Network of Global Corporate Control', *PLoS One* 6.10 (October 2011), pp. 1–6.

For an enlightening examination of the combined impact of economic globalization and digital technology on the global work environment, see Richard Baldwin, *The Globotics Upheaval: Globalization, Robotics, and the Future of Work* (Oxford University Press, 2020).

Chapter 4: The political dimension of globalization

The best introduction to political globalization is John Baylis and Steve Smith, *The Globalization of World Politics*, 8th edn (Oxford University Press, 2020).

For the arguments of hyperglobalizers, see Kenichi Ohmae, *The End of the Nation-State* (Free Press, 1995); and Thomas Friedman, *The Lexus and the Olive Tree: Understanding Globalization* (Farrar Straus Giroux, 1999). For the position of the globalization sceptics, see Paul Hirst, Grahame Thompson, and Simon Bromley, *Globalization in Question*, 3rd edn (Polity, 2009).

For the complete Mueller Report, see Robert S. Mueller III, 'Report on the Investigation into Russian Interference in the 2016 Presidential Election', Washington, DC, March 2019, p. 1; <https://www.justice.gov/storage/report.pdf >.

David Held's elements of cosmopolitan democracy are taken from Daniele Archibugi and David Held, eds, *Cosmopolitan Democracy* (Polity Press, 1995), pp. 96–120.

Chapter 5: The cultural dimension of globalization

For a comprehensive study on the cultural dimensions of globalization, see Jan Nederveen Pieterse, *Globalization and Culture: Global Melange*, 4th edn (Rowman & Littlefield, 2019).

For the arguments of pessimistic globalizers, see Benjamin Barber, *Consumed* (W. W. Norton and Company, 2007). For the arguments of optimistic globalizers, see Thomas L. Friedman, *The World Is Flat 3.0: A Brief History of the Twenty-First Century* (Picador, 2007). For the arguments of the sceptics, see Arjun Appadurai, *Modernity at Large* (University of Minnesota Press, 1996).

For the pivotal role of the global media, see Jack Lule, *Globalization and the Media: Global Village of Babel*, 4th edn (Rowman & Littlefield, 2021).

On English as a global language, see Robert McCrum, *Globish: How the English Language Became the World's Language* (W. W. Norton, 2010).

For the most-used languages on the Internet, see Govind Bhutada, 'Visualizing the Most Used Languages on the Internet' (2021), <https://www.visualcapitalist.com/the-most-used-languages-on-the-internet/>.

Chapter 6: The ecological dimension of globalization

An accessible yet comprehensive book on ecological globalization is Peter Christoff and Robyn Eckersley, *Globalization and the Environment* (Rowman & Littlefield, 2013).

For a concise explanation of the 'Anthropocene' concept, see Erle C. Ellis, *Anthropocene: A Very Short Introduction* (Oxford University Press, 2018).

For a comprehensive yet accessible overview of global climate change issues that also effectively debunks the myths of climate change deniers, see Robert Henson, *A Thinking Person's Guide to Climate Change*, 2nd edn (American Meteorological Society, 2019).

The three UN Reports are: (1) UNIPCC (2018), *Global Warming of 1.5°C* report: <http://www.ipcc.ch/report/sr15/>; (2) UNIPCC (2022), *Impact, Adaptation, and Vulnerability* report: <https://www.ipcc.ch/report/sixth-assessment-report-working-group-ii/>; (3) UNIPCC (2022), *Mitigation of Climate Change*: <https://www.ipcc.ch/report/sixth-assessment-report-working-group-3/>.

The excerpt of Pope Francis's climate appeal has been taken from *Laudato Si* ('Praise Be to You'), Encyclical Letter issued by Pope Francis I on 24 May 2015, <https://www.vatican.va/content/francesco/en/encyclicals/documents/papa-francesco_20150524_enciclica-laudato-si.html>.

Chapter 7: Ideological confrontations over globalization

For a more detailed account of the ideological dimensions of globalization, see Manfred B. Steger, *The Rise of the Global Imaginary: Political Ideologies from the French Revolution to the Global War on Terror* (Oxford University Press, 2009); and *Globalisms: Facing the Populist Challenge*, 4th edn (Rowman & Littlefield, 2020).

A readable account of globalization from a market globalist perspective can be found in Jagdish Bhagwati, *In Defense of Globalization* (Oxford University Press, 2007).

The justice-globalist claims and information on the global justice movement in general can be found in: Manfred B. Steger, James Goodman, and Erin K. Wilson, *Justice Globalism: Ideology, Crises, Policy* (Sage, 2013).

Two excellent academic treatments of jihadist globalism and its affiliated movements can be found in: Olivier Roy, *Globalized Islam: The Search for the New Ummah* (Columbia University Press, 2006) and Roel Meijer, *Global Salafism: Islam's New Religious Movement* (Oxford University Press, 2014).

My quotations from Donald Trump's public remarks were taken from two sources: (a) the American Presidency Project website: <http://presidency.ucsb.edu/2016_election.php>, an authoritative archive for the study of presidential speeches; and (b) the Factbase website: <http://factba.se>, a useful online source for the study of Trump's speeches, tweets, and video materials.

For an accessible overview of populism, see Cas Mudde and Cristobal Rovira Kaltwasser, *Populism: A Very Short Introduction* (Oxford University Press, 2017).

Chapter 8: Present and future trends

The excerpt appearing in the box 'Schwab on Globalization 4.0' is taken from Klaus Schwab, 'The New Architecture for the Fourth Industrial Revolution', *Foreign Affairs*, 16 January 2019; < https://www.foreignaffairs.com/articles/world/2019-01-16/globalization-40/>.

For a fascinating examination of the future of disembodied globalization and automation, see Richard Baldwin, *The Globotics Upheaval: Globalization, Robotics, and the Future of Work* (Oxford University Press, 2019).

The excerpt appearing in the box 'The dark side of Globalization 4.0' is taken from Shoshana Zuboff, *The Age of Surveillance Capitalism: The Fight for a Human Future at the New Frontier of Power* (Public Affairs, 2019), p. 9.

For a more comprehensive assessment of current and future globalization trends, see Manfred B. Steger and Paul James, *Globalization Matters: Engaging the Global in Unsettled Times* (Cambridge University Press, 2019).

Index

For the benefit of digital users, indexed terms that span two pages (e.g., 52–53) may, on occasion, appear on only one of those pages.

Globalization

INTERNATIONAL RELATIONS
A Very Short Introduction
Paul Wilkinson

Of undoubtable relevance today, in a post-9-11 world of growing political tension and unease, this *Very Short Introduction* covers the topics essential to an understanding of modern international relations. Paul Wilkinson explains the theories and the practice that underlies the subject, and investigates issues ranging from foreign policy, arms control, and terrorism, to the environment and world poverty. He examines the role of organizations such as the United Nations and the European Union, as well as the influence of ethnic and religious movements and terrorist groups which also play a role in shaping the way states and governments interact. This up-to-date book is required reading for those seeking a new perspective to help untangle and decipher international events.

www.oup.com/vsi

DIPLOMACY
A Very Short Introduction
Joseph M. Siracusa

Like making war, diplomacy has been around a very long time, at least since the Bronze Age. It was primitive by today's standards, there were few rules, but it was a recognizable form of diplomacy. Since then, diplomacy has evolved greatly, coming to mean different things, to different persons, at different times, ranging from the elegant to the inelegant. Whatever one's definition, few could doubt that the course and consequences of the major events of modern international diplomacy have shaped and changed the global world in which we live. Joseph M. Siracusa introduces the subject of diplomacy from a historical perspective, providing examples from significant historical phases and episodes to illustrate the art of diplomacy in action.

'Professor Siracusa provides a lively introduction to diplomacy through the perspective of history.'

Gerry Woodard, Senior Fellow in Political Science at the University of Melbourne and former Australasian Ambassador in Asia

GEOPOLITICS
A Very Short Introduction
Klaus Dodds

In certain places such as Iraq or Lebanon, moving a few
feet either side of a territorial boundary can be a matter of life
or death, dramatically highlighting the connections between
place and politics. For a country's location and size as well as
its sovereignty and resources all affect how the people that live
there understand and interact with the wider world. Using
wide-ranging examples, from historical maps to James Bond
films and the rhetoric of political leaders like Churchill and
George W. Bush, this Very Short Introduction shows why,
for a full understanding of contemporary global politics, it is
not just smart - it is essential - to be geopolitical.

'Engrossing study of a complex topic.'

Mick Herron, Geographical.

INTERNATIONAL MIGRATION
A Very Short Introduction
Khalid Koser

Why has international migration become an issue of such intense public and political concern? How closely linked are migrants with terrorist organizations? What factors lie behind the dramatic increase in the number of women migrating? This *Very Short Introduction* examines the phenomenon of international human migration - both legal and illegal. Taking a global look at politics, economics, and globalization, the author presents the human side of topics such as asylum and refugees, human trafficking, migrant smuggling, development, and the international labour force.

www.oup.com/vsi

Citizenship
A Very Short Introduction
Richard Bellamy

Interest in citizenship has never been higher. But what does it mean to be a citizen of a modern, complex community? Why is citizenship important? Can we create citizenship, and can we test for it? In this fascinating Very Short Introduction, Richard Bellamy explores the answers to these questions and more in a clear and accessible way. He approaches the subject from a political perspective, to address the complexities behind the major topical issues. Discussing the main models of citizenship, exploring how ideas of citizenship have changed through time from ancient Greece to the present, and examining notions of rights and democracy, he reveals the irreducibly political nature of citizenship today.

'Citizenship is a vast subject for a short introduction, but Richard Bellamy has risen to the challenge with aplomb.'

Mark Garnett, TLS

www.oup.com/vsi

THE EUROPEAN UNION

A Very Short Introduction

John Pinder & Simon Usherwood

This *Very Short Introduction* explains the European Union in plain English. Fully updated for 2007 to include controversial and current topics such as the Euro currency, the EU's enlargement, and its role in ongoing world affairs, this accessible guide shows how and why the EU has developed from 1950 to the present. Covering a range of topics from the Union's early history and the ongoing interplay between 'eurosceptics' and federalists, to the single market, agriculture, and the environment, the authors examine the successes and failures of the EU, and explain the choices that lie ahead in the 21st century.

The United Nations
A Very Short Introduction
Jussi M. Hanhimäki

With this much-needed introduction to the UN, Jussi Hanhimäki
engages the current debate over the organization's effectiveness
as he provides a clear understanding of how it was originally
conceived, how it has come to its present form, and how it
must confront new challenges in a rapidly changing world. After
a brief history of the United Nations and its predecessor, the
League of Nations, the author examines the UN's successes
and failures as a guardian of international peace and security,
as a promoter of human rights, as a protector of international law,
and as an engineer of socio-economic development.

www.oup.com/vsi

NEOLIBERALISM
A Very Short Introduction
Manfred B. Steger & Ravi K. Roy

Anchored in the principles of the free-market economics, 'neoliberalism' has been associated with such different political leaders as Ronald Reagan, Margaret Thatcher, Bill Clinton, Tony Blair, Augusto Pinochet, and Junichiro Koizumi.So is neoliberalism doomed or will it regain its former glory? Will reform-minded G-20 leaders embark on a genuine new course or try to claw their way back to the neoliberal glory days of the Roaring Nineties? Is there a viable alternative to neoliberalism? Exploring the origins, core claims, and considerable variations of neoliberalism, this Very Short Introduction offers a concise and accessible introduction to one of the most debated 'isms' of our time.

'This book is a timely and relevant contribution to this urgent contemporary topic.'

I. K. Gujral, Former Prime Minister of India

Economics
A Very Short Introduction
Partha Dasgupta

Economics has the capacity to offer us deep insights into some of the most formidable problems of life, and offer solutions to them too. Combining a global approach with examples from everyday life, Partha Dasgupta describes the lives of two children who live very different lives in different parts of the world: in the Mid-West USA and in Ethiopia. He compares the obstacles facing them, and the processes that shape their lives, their families, and their futures. He shows how economics uncovers these processes, finds explanations for them, and how it forms policies and solutions.

'An excellent introduction ... presents mathematical and statistical findings in straightforward prose.'

Financial Times